Rural Agriculture Marketing

Indian Council of Agricultural Research (ICAR)

Dr. Balasaheb Sawant Konkan Krishi Vidyapeeth (DBSKKV)

National Agricultural Higher Education Project-Institutional Development Plan (NAHEP-IDP)

NIPA® Genx Electronic Resources & Solutions P. Ltd., New Delhi-110 034

About the Authors

Dr. Anil R. Pande is well known educator, researcher in the field of marketing management and general management. He is winner of numerous prestigious awards, including best researcher during his vist to Thailand for attending research conference. He is also author of dozens of academic research publications. He has in all 22 years of teaching experience. He is PhD guide and work in capacity of Associate Professor and Coordinator for Part Time Masters course at Jamnalal bajaj Institute of Management Studies, University of Mumbai.

Snehal A. Khanvilkar is a dynamic professional and dedicated research scholar specializing in Management. Currently holding the position of Young Professional – II at NAHEP-IDP, Dr. DBSKKV, Dapoli, she is deeply committed to institutional development, enhancing learning outcomes, and fostering academic diversity, entrepreneurship, and employability.

With a Master's in Management Studies (MMS) with a focus on Operations and a Bachelor's in Food Technology, she possesses a strong academic foundation.

She has a professional journey that includes roles as an Assistant Professor at Vishwabhushan Bharatratna Dr. Babasaheb Ambedkar (Model) College, Guest Lecturer, and internships in diverse industries such as Mondelez International, Britannia, Mahananda Company, Vinsura Wineyard, and Weikfield Pvt. Ltd.

Beyond academic and professional achievements, she has showcased leadership skills as the Head of Department for National Service Scheme, Cultural, and Women Empowerment at Vishwabhushan Bharatratna Dr. Babasaheb Ambedkar (Model) College. Notably, Snehal represented the University of Mumbai as the Team Manager at the "AVHAN-2019" State level Disaster Management Camp under NDRF.

In pursuit of continuous learning and expertise enhancement, she is currently pursuing a Ph.D. in Management. The author has earned certifications in Internal Auditing of ISO 22000:2009, HACCP, and training from prominent companies like Mondelez International, Weikfield Pvt. Ltd., Britannia, Mahananda Dairy, and Vinsura Wineyard.

She has a research acumen is evident through winning the Best Research Paper Award at an international conference.she has been involved in various projects, including Operation and Production Technology at Mondelez International (Cadbury Company) and ongoing research on the application of supply chain management in the Konkan region.

Possessing a diverse skill set, she is excels in internal auditing, 5S implementation, new product development (NPD), corrective and preventive action (CAPA) reports, ISO/TS documentation, MoU documentation, machine operation in the food industry, product conceptualization, team leadership, procurement-related documentation, event management, quality management system (QMS) implementation, project management, strategic planning, and collaboration. she is undoubtedly a multifaceted professional poised for significant contributions in the fields of Operations, Total Quality Management, R&D, and more.

Rural Agriculture Marketing

Compiled by

Prashant S. Bodake
Dean & Director of Instruction, DBSKKV
Co-ordinator & Principal Investigator
NAHEP-IDP, DBSKKV-Dapoli, Maharashtra

Srinivasan Iyengar
Director of Jamnalal Bajaj Institute of Management Studies
Mumbai, Maharashtra

Prakash J.Kshirsagar
Co-Chair, AGRIC-CITTL
NAHEP-IDP, DBSKKV-Dapoli, Maharashtra

Authors

Anil Pande
Associate Professor
JBIMS
University of Mumbai, Maharashtra

Snehal A. Khanvilkar
Young Professional-II-Management
DBSKKV, Dapoli, Maharashtra

Indian Council of Agricultural Research (ICAR)

Dr. Balasaheb Sawant Konkan Krishi Vidyapeeth (DBSKKV)

National Agricultural Higher Education Project-Institutional Development Plan (NAHEP-IDP)

NIPA® Genx Electronic Resources & Solutions P. Ltd., New Delhi-110 034

Citation: National Agriculture Higher Education Project Institutional Development Plan, DBSKKV, Dapoli & ICAR, New Delhi

NIPA® GENX ELECTRONIC RESOURCES & SOLUTIONS P. LTD.

101,103, Vikas Surya Plaza, CU Block
L.S.C.Market, Pitam Pura, New Delhi-110 034
Ph : +91 11 27341616, 27341717, 27341718
E-mail: newindiapublishingagency@gmail.com
Website: www.nipabooks.com

For customer assistance, please contact
Phone: + 91-11-27 34 17 17
Fax: + 91-11-27 34 16 16

ISBN: 978-93-58870-97-8

Composed and Designed by NIPA®.

भारतीय कृषि अनुसंधान परिषद
कृषि अनुसंधान भवन-II, नई दिल्ली-110012
INDIAN COUNCIL OF AGRICULTURAL RESEARCH
KRISHI ANUSANDHAN BHAVAN-II, PUSA, NEW DELHI-110012
Phone: +91-11-25841760
Email: ddg.edu@icar.gov.in, ddgedn@gmail.com, nd.nahep@icar.gov.in

Dr. Rakesh Chandra Agrawal
Deputy Director General (Agril. Edn.)

Message

It is with immense pleasure and a sense of purpose that I provide this forward to the National Agricultural Higher Education Project-Institutional Development Plan (NAHEP-IDP) at Dr. Balasaheb Sawant Konkan Krishi Vidyapeeth (DBSKKV) and the concurrent endeavour to develop a short pilot course in skilling small-scale agri-entrepreneurship. This transformative initiative is under the guidance and leadership of the Hon'ble Vice Chancellor of DBSKKV Dr.S.G.Bhave.

Principal Investigator of NAHEP-IDP, DBSKKV-Dapoli Dr. P.S.Bodake, a distinguished and visionary leader in the field of agriculture, has consistently championed the cause of advancing agricultural education, research, and extension services. His strategic vision has played a pivotal role in shaping the trajectory of agricultural development in our nation, with a keen focus on empowering farming communities and fostering innovation.

The NAHEP-IDP of DBSKKV stands as a testament to ICAR & World Bank commitment to elevating the standards of agricultural education. By providing institutional support and promoting excellence across various facets of academia, research, and extension activities, the project aims to position DBSKKV as a center of excellence in agricultural learning and research.

In tandem with the NAHEP-IDP, the initiation of a short pilot course in skilling smallscale agri-entrepreneurship reflects DBSKKV foresight in addressing contemporary challenges in agriculture. Recognizing the pivotal role played by small-scale agri-entrepreneurs in driving rural economies, this course is designed to equip them with the necessary skills and knowledge to navigate the dynamic landscape of agribusiness.

The NAHEP-IDP, DBSKKV envisions this pilot course as a stepping stone toward fostering a culture of entrepreneurship in agriculture. By blending theoretical insights with practical applications, the course seeks to empower agri-entrepreneurs, enabling them to adopt sustainable farming practices, embrace innovation, and contribute significantly to the economic prosperity of their communities.

I extend my heartfelt appreciation to Dr. P.S. Bodake and his entire NAHEP-IDP Team for their steadfast leadership and unwavering commitment to advancing agricultural education and entrepreneurship. Under his guidance, these initiatives are poised to make a lasting impact on the agricultural education landscape and the entrepreneurial spirit within the students and farming community.

(R.C. Agrawal)
Deputy Director General (Agril. Edn.)

DR. BALASAHEB SAWANT KONKAN KRISHI VIDYAPEETH
Dapoli, Dist. Ratnagiri - 415712
Tel. No.: (0)02358-282064, **Fax No.**: 02358-282074, **Mob.**: 9422556565
E-mail : vcdbskkv-mh@gov.in, ipmbhave@gmail.com, **website** : www.dbskkv.org

Dr. Sanjay G. Bhave
IDP Leader
Vice Chancellor, DBSKKV

Foreword

I am delighted to present the Institutional Development Plan as part of the National Agricultural Higher Education Project (NAHEP) undertaken by our esteemed institution. This initiative marks a significant milestone in our commitment to advancing agricultural education, research, and innovation, with the ultimate goal of transforming the agricultural landscape of our nation.

This pilot course serves as a testament to our university's dedication to fostering innovation and fostering collaboration between academia and industry. We believe that by offering this course, we are not only contributing to the skill development of individuals but also playing a pivotal role in shaping the future of agriculture.

We, at DBSKKV are happy to felicitate the proficient attainment of the Principal Investigator, IDP Coordinator, and Dean and Director of Instruction of DBSKKV-Dr.Prashant S. Bodake and team NAHEP-IDP involved in the same vertical. Your magnificent work makes all of us highly gratified and prosperous. Well Done!

I extend my gratitude to the faculty members, industry experts, and stakeholders who have contributed their expertise and insights to the development of this course. Their collective efforts have ensured that the curriculum aligns with the ever-changing demands of the agricultural sector.

I am excited to witness the impact that this short pilot course on skilling small-scale agricultural entrepreneurship will have on our participants and, consequently, on the agricultural landscape. With this initiative, we are sowing the seeds of empowerment and innovation, cultivating a new generation of agripreneurs who will not only navigate challenges but also unearth opportunities for growth.

(Sanjay G. Bhave)
IDP Leader
Vice Chancellor, DBSKKV

NATIONAL AGRICULTURAL HIGHER EDUCATION PROJECT
AGRICULTURAL EDUCATION DIVISION
INDIAN COUNCIL OF AGRICULTURAL RESEARCH
(Department of Agricultural Research and Education
Ministry of Agriculture and Farmers Welfare, Government of India)
Room No. 514, Krishi Anusandhan Bhawan-II, Pusa, New Delhi-110 012

Date : 14.12.2023

Dr. N.K. Jain
National Coordinator (IDP)

Message

It is a matter of great pleasure to learn that Dr. Balasaheb Sawant Konkan Krishi Vidyapeeth, Dapoli has developed short pilot course on "Skilling Small-scale Agri-Entrepreneurship" for the undergraduate students. The efforts made by DBSKKV, Dapoli and the Knowledge Experts is a significant stride towards fostering interdisciplinary learning and preparing students for the evolving landscape of agriculture. Agriculture, the backbone of our nation, is undergoing a transformative phase that demands a comprehensive understanding of not only traditional farming practices but also entrepreneurial skills. In this context, DBSKKV, Dapoli is driven by the vision to equip undergraduate students with the knowledge and skills necessary to navigate the complexities of modern agriculture and contribute to the burgeoning field of agri-entrepreneurship. I commend the leadership of Dr. S.G. Bhave, Hon'ble Vice Chancellor, DBSKVV, Dapoli for his forward-thinking approach in embracing this initiative and commitment to provide a robust academic environment aligns seamlessly with our objective of preparing students for the dynamic and competitive landscape of agriculture and entrepreneurship.

I also congratulate Dr. P.S. Bodake, Principal Investigator of NAHEP-IDP, DBSKKV, Dapoli and his entire team, whose collaborative efforts have been instrumental in shaping the curriculum of this course. Together, we envision a program that not only imparts knowledge but also nurtures a spirit of inquiry and enterprise among the students. I extend my warmest congratulations to the University on the launch of the innovative short pilot course on "Skilling Small-scale Agri-Entrepreneurship". May this endeavour be a beacon of progress, fostering excellence in agricultural education and empowering the next generation of agri-entrepreneurs. University's commitment to bridging theory and practical is commendable, and I am confident that this initiative will contribute significantly to the growth of our agricultural landscape.

Place: New Delhi

(N. K. Jain)

NATIONAL AGRICULTURE HIGHER EDUCATION PROJECT INSTITUTIONAL DEVELOPMENT PLAN
DR. BALASAHEB SAWANT KONKAN KRISHI VIDYAPEETH,
DAPOLI, DIST. RATNAGIRI
Mob. No.: 9420413255 / 8275201130
Email.: (P)prameghash@gmail.com (O) hodagrodapoli@gmail.com (O) piidpdbskkv@gmail.com (O)nodalcelldbskkv@gmail.com

Dr. P. S. Bodake
Dean & Director of Instruction
Coordinator, Principal Investigator, NAHEP-IDP

Message

It is with immense pride and anticipation that I present the Institutional Development Plan as part of our active involvement in the National Agricultural Higher Education Project (NAHEP). This plan embodies our institution's unwavering commitment to redefining agricultural education and research, and it signifies a transformative journey towards excellence and innovation.

Through this plan, we aim to enhance our institutional capacities, bolster research initiatives, and cultivate strategic partnerships with industries and communities. By incorporating modern pedagogical techniques, fostering interdisciplinary collaboration, and harnessing the potential of emerging technologies, we strive to create a learning ecosystem that empowers our students to become leaders and change-makers in the agricultural sector and it will not only elevate our institution's stature but also propel the agricultural education and research landscape towards a brighter and more sustainable future.

Our joint commitment to education and empowerment has culminated in the creation of this pilot course. Through a harmonious blend of theoretical insights and practical experiences, participants will delve into market trends, value chain analysis, sustainable practices, financial management, and the integration of technology into agriculture. This holistic approach is designed to prepare individuals to navigate the intricacies of agripreneurship with confidence.

This pilot course is an embodiment of our dedication to fostering collaboration between academia and industry. By bridging the gap between theory and practice, we aim to nurture a new generation of agripreneurs who are poised to steer the agricultural sector towards innovation and growth.

We sincerely mention primitive gratitude towards the former Vice-chancellor of DBSKKV Dr. Sanjay D. Sawant and Vice-chancellor of DBSKKV Dr. Sanjay G. Bhave for such prudent leadership and providence. We feel proud to highlight the sheer hard work and great dedication of the Co-Principal Investigator of NAHEP-IDP and IDP Staff.

We are grateful to the Director of Jamnalal Bajaj Institute of Management-Mumbai Dr. Shrinivasan Iyengar for such excellent association and cordial congruence in the course of developing a short pilot course in skilling small-scale Agri-Entrepreneurship. We also express our sincere gratitude to the faculty members of JBIMS & University of Mumbai, industry experts, and stakeholders whose expertise and contributions have shaped this course. Their collective wisdom ensures that the curriculum remains attuned to the evolving demands of the agricultural landscape.

Thank you.

(P. S. Bodake)
Dean & Director of Instruction
Coordinator, Principal Investigator, NAHEP-IDP

Preface

Agricultural Marketing Management encompasses the strategic planning, execution, and control of activities involved in the efficient movement of agricultural products from producers to consumers. In this context, marketing management refers to the application of principles and practices to optimize the marketing of agricultural goods. The rural marketing environment plays a crucial role, shaped by factors such as infrastructure, government policies, and socio-economic conditions. Understanding consumer behaviour in rural areas is essential, considering the unique characteristics of rural products and the distinct preferences of consumers. Examining the recent market scenario in India provides insights into the dynamic nature of agricultural marketing, reflecting changes in demand, supply chains, and policy influences that impact the overall landscape.

This book focuses on the intersection of Rural Market Strategies and the Consumer Decision-Making Process, emphasizing key elements that shape marketing dynamics in rural areas. It explores Rural Marketing Strategies, delving into tailored approaches that account for the unique challenges and opportunities present in rural markets. The discussion then shifts to consumer buying behaviour, examining the intricacies of decision-making processes in rural contexts. Technological and economic factors play a pivotal role in shaping consumer preferences, and the subject underscores their significance in the rural market landscape. Additionally, the impact of the marketing environment on consumer choices is explored, providing insights into how external factors influence purchasing decisions. Finally, the book touches on the role of innovation and diffusion in rural markets, highlighting their importance in shaping strategies that resonate with the specific needs and preferences of rural consumers.

This book delves into the intricacies of Rural Distribution Systems, exploring key components and their impact on the efficient flow of goods in rural markets. It begins by examining the concept and nature of distribution, emphasizing the unique challenges and characteristics associated with rural distribution networks. The subject then differentiates distribution strategies for consumer and industrial goods in rural contexts, highlighting the diverse considerations in these sectors. Rural Market Segmentation is explored as a critical aspect, acknowledging the need for nuanced approaches tailored to the specific demographics and preferences of rural consumers. Additionally, the book touches on the interplay between rural communication and distribution systems, recognizing the interconnectedness of effective communication in facilitating efficient distribution. The role of Agricultural Produce Marketing Committees is discussed, underscoring their significance in regulating and optimizing the distribution of agricultural products in rural areas.

This book explores the role of Information Communication & Technology (ICT) in the context of Rural Marketing, with a focus on key aspects and tools. It begins by examining Marketing Communications and Channels, emphasizing the pivotal role of effective communication in rural marketing strategies. Determining Marketing Communication Objectives is then discussed, highlighting the importance of clear objectives to guide communication efforts in reaching rural audiences. The subject content also explores the role of Social Marketing in the marketing of rural goods, recognizing the influence of social platforms in shaping consumer perceptions and behaviours. Information Technology and Communication in Rural Marketing are discussed as essential components, showcasing how technological advancements contribute to the optimization of marketing efforts in rural areas. Finally, the subject highlights specific tools such as eNAM and AGMARKNET, illustrating their significance as Information Communication & Technology tools that play a crucial role in enhancing the efficiency and transparency of rural marketing processes.

This book focuses on Market Support in the context of rural marketing, highlighting key elements that contribute to the development and sustenance of rural markets. It begins by exploring Rural Marketing Research and Techniques, emphasizing the importance of informed decision-making through comprehensive research methods tailored to rural environments. The Rural Marketing Information System is discussed as a crucial component, acknowledging the significance of timely and accurate information for effective market support. Sources of Rural Credit are explored, recognizing the role of financial support in empowering rural businesses and consumers. The book also sheds light on the pivotal role of financial institutions like NABARD (National Bank for Agriculture and Rural Development) in fostering rural development through credit and financial services. Finally, it touches upon the concept of Corporate Social Responsibility in Rural Marketing, underscoring the responsibility of corporations in contributing to the sustainable development of rural communities.

Authors

Contents

1

Rural Marketing

Introduction

Agriculture marketing and Rural marketing are two words used interchangeably by the people at large with the study of agriculture and management discipline. India is known to the world for its agricultural growth through the green revolution. India is an agriculture-based and oriented economy with approximately six and a half lakh villages predominantly involved in agricultural and agri-based activities. Rural India is termed as the backbone of the Indian economy and it contributes significantly to the economy and to its GDP (Gross Domestic Product) in terms of providing food grains (Cereals and Pulses), vegetables, and fruits which are essential ingredients for human life.

Approximately 60% of the Indian population lives in rural areas and depends directly or indirectly on agriculture and allied activities such as dairy, poultry and pisciculture and also life based on these industries. Rural agricultural products, products made by tiny industries and specially hand made products and produces are in great demand in the cities and urban areas. Rural products like handlooms and handicrafts are very popular among foreign tourists. With opening up of the Indian economy to the competition and also with advent of tremendous demand created with the invasion of technology and internet, many rural organizations have started professionally operating their organizations with a better understanding of the functions of management and the concepts of rural marketing.

The rural marketing is not only the subject of study in educational institutions but also has grown as an area of practice, livelihood with agricultural and allied activities. The accomplishments of Self-help Groups, Micro Finance Institutions, Farmers Interest Groups, Rural artisans' businesses, and Farmers producer organisations have to be given due credit in the growth of rural organizations. Having all lucrative side allurements, the rural marketing with agricultural marketing do pose different types of challenges to the marketers and managers. The challenges are primarily due to the absence of a proper framework to guide decision making in rural markets. In recent years a lot of work has been undertaken in the area of rural marketing and new concepts, definitions and technological advancements have been incorporated for better understanding of rural marketing. An estimated 71% of rural consumers choose branded products over unbranded products, and approximately 66% of rural consumers give weightage to brand image, functionality and aesthetics while making purchase decisions. Rural marketers can tap this opportunity which would help them in gaining long term competitive advantage. Let's understand Rural marketing from the perspective of managers and let's try to have hands-ons on experience while learning it by practicing.

2

Rural Marketing Management

Introduction

India is known for its heritage and diaspora has 6,40,867 villages with a population of aprox 120 crore people which is about 66.46 % of the population. The villages in India have always remained neglected and never tried to market their products to urban consumers. But the rise in incomes of the Indian urban consumers and the increased awareness due to technological advancement it leads to the growth of the Indian consumer market which became attractive for the Indian as well as foreign companies. The efforts by Indian Government for rural products contributed to the development of rural products and their marketing. A shift from an agricultural economy to a service economy resulted in the growth of job opportunities and created a demand for goods and services by consumers. Earlier the rural market was dependent on urban marketers for their requirements like seeds, fertilizers, pesticides, cattle feed and agricultural machinery, but the scenario has changed now that rural products have been largely accepted by the urban consumers also. According to NCAER report over seventy percent of bicycles, mechanical watches and transistors and about sixty percent of batteries, sewing machines and table fans are sold in rural India. The rural producers now become more conscious about marketing their products to urban consumers and rural marketers are trying out innovative ways to approach the urban markets. While rural products offer tremendous opportunities for marketers, it is not easy to enter the urban markets due to cut-throat competition in the urban markets. Hence understanding the purchase behaviour of the consumers become important for the marketer and for this effective market research is indispensable for effective formulation of marketing strategies. Offering better quality of life for the rural population will be the next role of the companies. Thus, marketing of rural products offers opportunities and challenges for marketers. The market strategy formulation includes understanding the behavior of urban consumers and the formulation of the marketing mix as per the requirement of the urban markets. A better understanding of consumer behavior helps companies to better satisfy their customers. Since the urban markets have more disposable incomes and better life styles therefore the scope for marketing the rural products to the urban consumers is very high.

• Definitions

Rural and Urban

Rural: The NSSO defines rural as any territory which has population density of upto 400per km^2, have no municipal board and minimum 75% of male working population is involved in agriculture and allied activities. The definition of rural is closely tied with the urban definition which is as follows:

Urban: the term urban has been defined as:

1. All places having a municipality, corporation, cantonment board etc
2. All places having a minimum population of 5000 and atleast 75 of the population in engaged in non-agricultural activities; and
3. An area where density of population is at least 400 persons per sq. km.

• Definition: Marketing Management

According to **American Marketing Association (AMA)**

Marketing is creating, communicating, delivering and exchanging offerings that have value to clients, customers and society at large.

Marketing management is the way to find out the opportunities which are profitable and create these opportunities by satisfying the customers.

Marketing management is a process of controlling the marketing aspects, setting the goals of a company, organizing the plans step by step, taking decisions for the firm, and executing them to get the maximum turn over by meeting the consumers' demands.

Philip Kotler has defined Marketing management as the art and science of choosing target markets and getting, keeping and growing customers through creating, delivering and communicating superior customer values of management.

India is a land of diversity, and different dialects and around 60% percent of the Indian population lives in villages. Villages help in economic development through the production of food grains, vegetables, fruits, etc. The export of these agricultural products results in the earnings of much needed foreign exchange. The size of the Indian rural market is vast and scattered and has a strong base. The rural market comprises about 66.66% of the Indian population which has immense potential in terms of providing products to the urban markets which have higher disposable incomes. The understanding of consumer behavior is of utmost importance for rural marketers as it gives insight into the unsatisfied needs and behavior patterns of urban consumers.

Hence, Rural marketing is concerned with the activities of assembling; grading, transportation, and distribution of goods from the company to the consumer. Rural marketing is an evolving concept, and companies have realized the importance of this huge untapped market. The companies have improved their infrastructure and reach, with the intent to go rural. With the liberalization, the consumers are aware about the brands available in the market.

AMA has recently reframed the definition for rural marketing, and hence **Rural marketing** can be defined as a process of planning, and executing the conception, pricing, promotion, and distribution of ideas, goods, and services to create exchange that satisfy individual and organizational objectives.

Rural marketing activities are undertaken in rural areas to satisfy rural segments.

Thus, rural marketing can be seen as a function which manages all those activities involved in assessing, influencing and converting the purchasing power into an effective demand for desired products and services, and providing them to the people in rural area to satisfy the consumers.

What is Marketing Management

Traditionally, markets were viewed as a place for exchange of goods and services between sellers and buyers to the mutual benefit of both. Marketing is an exchange of values between the seller and the buyer. Value implies worth related to the goods and services being exchanged. The buyer will be ready to pay for the goods if they have some value for him.

Marketing is the business function that controls the level and composition of demand in the market. It deals with creating and maintaining demand for goods and services of the organization.

Marketing management is "planning, organising, controlling and implementing of marketing programmes, policies, strategies and tactics designed to create and satisfy the demand for the firms' product offerings or services as a means of generating an acceptable profit."

It deals with creating and regulating the demand and providing goods to customers for which they are willing to pay a price worth their value.

Marketing Management performs all managerial functions in the field of marketing. Marketing Management identifies market opportunities and comes out with appropriate strategies for exploring those opportunities profitably. It has to implement marketing programme and evaluate continuously the effectiveness of marketing-mix. It has to remove the deficiencies observed in the actual execution of marketing plans, policies, and procedures. It looks after the marketing system of the enterprise.

According to Philip Kotler, "Marketing Management is the art and science of choosing target markets and building profitable relationship with them. Marketing management is a process involving analysis, planning, implementing and control and it covers goods, services, ideas and the goal is to produce satisfaction to the parties involved".

From the above definitions, we can conclude that Marketing Management is the process of management of marketing programmes for accomplishing organizational goals and objectives.

Marketing Management Involves

1. The setting of marketing goals and objectives,
2. Developing the marketing plan,
3. Organising the marketing function,
4. Putting the marketing plan into action and
5. Controlling the marketing programme.

Marketing Management Concept

Marketing Management is both a science as well as an art. Those responsible for marketing should have good understanding of the various concepts and practices in marketing, communication, and analytical skills and ability to maintain effective relationship with customers, which will enable them to plan and execute marketing plans.

Therefore, a manufacturer should design and manufacture a product which will be accepted by the consumer rather than the one which can be manufactured by him easily. A consumer is basically fastidious and fickle minded. This makes that task of understanding the consumer and designing an appropriate product much more difficult, however this is the only way a manufacturer can succeed in a competitive market.

Selling should be preceded by customer study, marketing research and product development. The entire focus should be on the consumer and his needs.

"The aim of marketing is to know and understand the consumer so well that that the product or service fits him and sells itself. marketing should result in a customer who is ready to buy. All that should be needed then is to make the product or service available" – Peter Drucker. This concept is also called customer orientation.

The marketing concept which is also called the modern marketing concept as practised by most of the firms in the present situation is actually a combination of all the other concepts. The modern marketing concept consists of an integrated effort on the part of the marketer to identify the consumer needs and satisfy them through appropriately designed products and for this task use all the marketing techniques related to product, selling, market study, consumer behavior, product designing, pricing etc.

"The Marketing concept is a customer orientation backed by integrated marketing aimed at generating customer satisfaction as the key to satisfying organizational goals". – Philip Kotler

"Modern marketing concept is a corporate state of mind that insists on the integration and co-ordination of all marketing functions which in turn are welded with the other corporate functions for the basic objective of producing maximum long range corporate profits." -Felton

The features of marketing concept: (modern marketing concept, integrated marketing concept, customer orientation)

i. Focus on customer needs – The needs of the consumer are studied and these become the basis of all product related activities such as designing, pricing, distribution, packaging etc.

ii. Providing consumer satisfaction – Every organization aims at providing maximum consumer satisfaction by understanding his needs and designing an appropriate product. The success of an organization is directly related to the consumer satisfaction it provides.

iii. Integrated Marketing Management – Marketing management is only a part of the total managerial functions of an organization such as finance management, production management, human resources management etc. All these functions are integrated in order to provide maximum satisfaction to the consumer. Thus all the functional areas of an organization are integrated.

iv. Achieving organizational goals – Modern marketing states that an organization must aim at maximizing consumer satisfaction and in the process enable itself to achieve its goals such as growth, market share and reasonable amount of profit or return on investment.

v. Innovation – Innovation is an important tool to provide consumer satisfaction. Innovative methods must be used to understand the consumer, design an appropriate product and offer it to the consumer

• Classification of Products

There are different types of products available in the market. Those are classified on the factors such as profitability, demand, competency of the company in making the product. Based on these parameters the products can be classified in to three categories:

- **Consumer and Industrial Products:** Consumer products are those products that are manufactured for the direct use of consumers such as toiletries, shampoos, food and beverages, cosmetics, etc. whereas Industrial products are those products that are used as raw materials for making the finished product .
- **Durables, Non-Durables and Services:** Durable goods are those tangible goods which survive many uses and non-durables goods are those goods which normally are consumed in one or a few uses. Services are intangible activities which have peculiar characteristics which make them different from tangible goods for example education, tourism, consultancy, banking, medical etc.
- **Convenience, Shopping and Specialty Goods:** These are the high involvement a product in the purchase of which considerable efforts is made. These are costly products which are bought once or twice in a life time. Convenience goods are those goods, which the consumer purchases frequently, with the minimum. These are also called as low involvement products. Shopping goods may require more shopping efforts on suitability, quality, price, and style parameters. Specialty goods have unique attributes for which the buyers are habitually willing to make a special purchasing effort. For example : Jewellery, House, a high end car etc
- **Unsought Goods**: Unsought goods are a part of convenience and speciality shopping with a difference that in these types of product the consumer is not interested to purchase and it requires strong selling efforts to sell these products. These types of products are called as unsought goods. E.g. Insurance

Organizations Strategies for Rural Markets

Most of the companies operating in India have reworked their marketing strategies formulated for the urban markets to suit the rural markets. All the elements of the marketing mix are tailored as per the requirements of the market.

This approach reflects marketer's efforts on the differing characteristics of rural markets and urban markets.

Rural markets are unique for the following reasons:

- The wants of rural consumers are not necessarily the same as those of urban consumers. These wants are shaped by a number of factors, including the environment.
- Social and cultural practices have an important influence on rural consumer behaviour. A marketer cannot ignore the influence of community on purchase behaviour
- The nature of occupation also influences the marketer's strategy. The popularity of small packs is a result of this.
- The political and economic institutions are significant for marketers. For example: Colgate- Palmolive, for example, uses the weekly village markets to promote its products.

Scope of Rural Marketing

Rural market exhibit immense scope in following respect

- Influential population: the urban population is 34.44% of the total population. This population is largely concentrated in cities. They have high disposable incomes. This urban population offers huge opportunities for rural products.
- Rising prosperity: The disposable income of urban consumers has considerably increased due to an increase in incomes and higher government salaries. Changes in lifestyles have influenced the behavior of urban consumers.
- Change in lifestyle: The lifestyle of urban consumers has changed considerably due to increased awareness and exposure facilitated by internet explosion.
- Market growth rate higher due to advanced technologies: The growth rate of fast-moving consumer goods (FMCG) and the durable

market is high in urban areas. Due to an increase in herbal products/ environmentally friendly products, the demand for rural products has increased considerably.

- Lifecycle changes: Applying the principle of the product life cycle the rural products which are in the introduction stage or growth stage can be targeted for the urban consumers.
- Rural marketing is not expensive: The expenditure for marketing of rural products in the markets is now affordable for the marketers due to the advent of social networking sites and cheap data.
- Attractive market for Agricultural and Milk Products: As the urban population is grappling with the problem of adulteration in milk products and Agricultural products therefore the rural marketers can provide unadulterated and fresh products to the consumers.

Marketing consists of two major areas, which are, marketing of agricultural products from rural to urban areas and marketing of manufactured goods and services in rural areas. Rural marketing is a two-way marketing process in which goods from rural markets are marketed in urban areas and goods and services from urban markets are marketed in rural areas. It also includes the flow of goods and services within the rural areas itself. The rural to urban transactions include agricultural products like food grains, oilseeds, cotton, sugarcane, tobacco, etc. The urban to rural transactions cover all the agricultural inputs and products like Fertilizers, pesticides, seeds, tractors, consumer durables like mobile phones, bicycles, laptops, and electrical and electronic items, and FMCG products. The processes of rural marketing are explained below:

1) **Urban to Rural:** Urban to rural transaction involves the selling of products and services by urban marketers in rural areas. These include Pesticides, Cars, Bikes Refrigerators, and Laptops etc.
2) **Rural to Urban:** In the rural to urban transaction a rural producer sells his agricultural produce in the urban market. This may be direct or indirect. In the direct transactions the rural marketer directly sells to the consumers in Mandis and Haats whereas in indirect transactions middlemen, agencies, government co-operatives, etc plays a pivotal role to sell agricultural products like fruits, vegetables, grains, pulses, handicrafts and others.
3) **Rural to Rural:** These include selling agricultural tools, products, cattle, carts and other agricultural products to another village in its proximity or within the rural areas like Sonpur mela in Bihar and Camel Fair in Pushkar etc.

• Rural Marketing Environment

Environment means the surroundings, influences or circumstances under which someone or something exists. According to Keith Davis the environment of any organization is "the aggregate of all conditions, events, and influences that surround and affect it". Environment has been divided into two major categories followed by sub-categories. Some of the different types of environment relevant to the study of rural marketing are as follows:

External Environment

1. Cultural and Economic
2. Economical
3. Technological
4. Political & Legal

PESTEL analysis is an important tool which describes a framework of macro-environmental factors used in the environmental scanning component of strategic management for formulating strategic decisions. A PESTEL analysis is an acronym for a tool used to identify the macro (external) forces facing an organisation. PESTEL stands for Political, Economic, Social, Technological, Environmental and Legal.

Internal Environment refers to the culture, members, events and factors within an organization that influences the decisions of the organization especially of its human resources.

Socio-Cultural

Rural areas in different states of India observe ladder of social strata. It is quite predominant in rural areas. Social customs are the behaviours which are expected of a particular culture. The caste systems in India are one of the examples of class structures in Indian societies. In the Indian societies the Gender Discrimination is a big problem which acknowledges that men and women are not equal. The cultural diversity in the Indian society means the existence of cultural and ethnic groups in a society. The socio cultural factors have a strong influence on the behaviour of the particular society. In such societies the reference groups plays an important role which have a strong influence on the purchase behaviours. The Indian socio cultural societies are also decided by religious beliefs which are the belief in the reality of the mythological aspects of a religion like poojas and rituals specific to socio cultural settings.

Economical Environment

Economic Environment is concerned with all the external economic factors that affects the buying behaviour of the customers therefore affect the overall performance of a company. These are uncontrollable factors which are beyond the control of the company the economic factors may be macro or Micro for example GDP, Purchasing power of the consumer.

Technological Environment

Technological Environment is the external factors in technology that impact business operation. Changes in technology affect the business operations. Due to this the business may have to dramatically change their operating strategy. This technological environment can help in increasing the reach of the product. The technological environment is responsible for three main revolutions:

1. Green revolution
2. White revolution

Examples: The latest technologies in the mobiles phones, fast productions, supply chains etc.

Political and Legal Environment

The Governments of a country want economic development of their country because of which they pass several rules and regulations to encourage business activity, the laws are put in place to control business activity and avoid undesirable outcomes. The regulations may be of different types and for different purpose, like Fiscal policy, Taxation Policy, GST, and demonetization.

The legal environment can be divided into different areas like:

1) Employment legislation
2) Environmental legislation
3) Consumer law
4) Competition law
5) Information /reporting law
6) Social legislation

• Product Life Cycle

The product is the core concept of the marketing which describes the different stages which the product undergoes. The main stages of the product life cycle are:

Introduction: In this the product is launchsed in the market.

- Growth: In this stage the sales of the product increases.
- Maturity: In this stage the sales starts to saturate.
- Decline: The final stage when the sales decline.

The product life cycle can be extended by activities mentioned as below:

- Advertising
- Price Discounts
- Value addition
- Exploring new markets
- Repositioning the product
- New Packaging

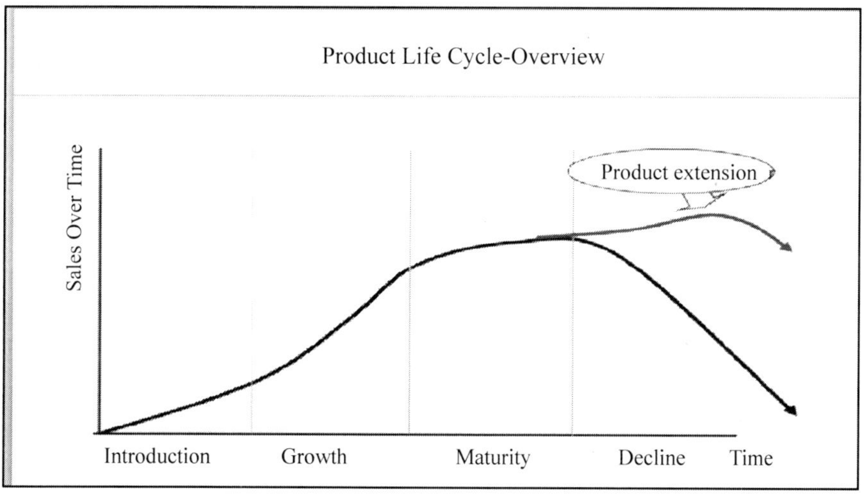

Fig.1.1: Product life cycle
Source: Raymond Vernon 1966

Consumer Markets Concept

Components of Consumer Markets

A market is a place where both the sellers and buyers meet. Certain conditions need to be fulfilled for the categorization of a place to be market. These conditions are both necessary and sufficient. These conditions may also be termed as the components of a market. These components as given by Payne, (1991) are as follows:

1. Availability of quality products for transactions the physical existence of a product is not necessary for some situations.
2. Existence of buyers and sellers. There should be a business relationship between buyers and sellers.
3. Demarcation of the area such as place, region, country or the whole world in the case of multinational corporations.
4. The existence of perfect competition or uniform pricing is not necessary.

A market is a physical place where buyers and sellers meet to buy and sell the goods. Traditionally markets can be classified on different bases like area, time, transactions, regulation, and volume of business, nature of goods, and nature of competition and demand and supply conditions. Economists describe a market as a collection buyers and sellers who transact over a particular product or product class. The figure given below diagrammatically represents the classification of consumer markets.

Rural market also can be classified on the basis of farm and non-farm sector of the economy.

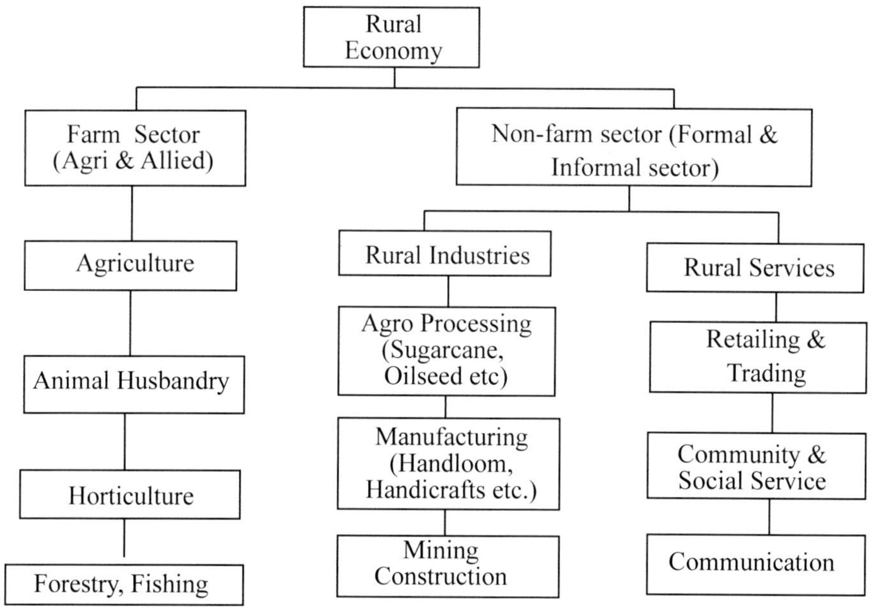

Fig. 1.2: Classification of Rural Marketing

Difference Between Rural and Urban Markets

The urban market is more evolved as compared to the rural market. The consumers are more exposed than their rural counterparts. Due to difference in both the markets in terms of major marketing variables, it is important to create different marketing strategies for the rural and urban markets. The two marketing strategies cannot be used interchangeably. Therefore rural marketing is different from the way marketing is planned and implemented in urban areas. Companies like HUL achieved success in the rural markets because of their structured marketing strategies for the rural markets in terms of planning and effort.

Rural markets exhibit prominent difference from urban markets in terms of

1. Availability of infrastructure
2. Lifestyle of the consumers
3. Context
4. Socio-cultural aspects
5. Demography, etc.

Rural Marketing Vs Urban Marketing

Differentiating Factors	Rural Markets	Urban Markets
Infrastructure Availability	Minimum provided	Maximum provided
Income Stream	Agricultural (seasonal, highly unreliable)	Non- Agricultural (Fixed Income ensured)
Lifestyle	Daily routines	Ever chainging
Context	Varies a lot	Varies a little
Social-Cultural Background	Value for money	Not exactly
Accessibility	Heterogeneous Markets, Logistics problem	Homongeneous, concentrated markets
Media reach in Habits	Varies a lot	Varies in little
Nature of competition	Less	Lot

Consumer Buyer Behaviour

Consumer buying process consists of sequential steps that the consumer follows to arrive at the final buying decisions. Mostly, consumers follow a typical buying process. Marketer must know how consumers reach the final decision to buy the product. Since, marketer is responsible for marketing and selling of goods in the market so the marketer must have the knowledge how the consumers actually make their buying decisions. In many cases the companies presume that consumer buying is random process.

There is a sequence of steps that most consumers go through before deciding whether to make a purchase or not? As discussed earlier there are various stages in the consumer buying behaviour which the customer undergoes purchasing the product. These stages can vary from consumers of urban to consumers of rural areas but normally the following steps are by and large followed by the consumer.

There are five stages to the consumer buying process and as a marketer if they can understand each stage in a comprehensive manner then they can market a product, offering or service to the consumers effectively.

Understanding consumer buying process enables the company to align the marketing strategy accordingly.

Therefore, the marketer must study the buying process from consumer's perspective. Company must take certain steps to support consumers in each stage to buy its product. The five stages framework is an important tool to evaluate the customer's buying process. John Dewey first introduced the following five stages in 1910. These steps are as follows:

1. Need Identification
2. Search for Information
3. Evaluation of alternatives
4. Final Purchase
5. Post-purchase behaviour

Diagrammatically the stages can be represented as follows:

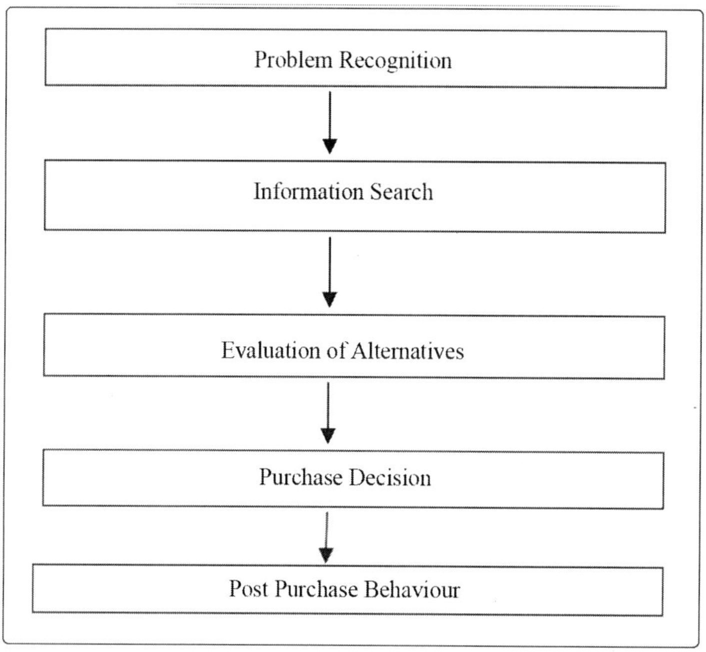

Fig. 1.3: Stages in consumer buying behaviour

1. **Need Identification**: The first and foremost step in the consumer buying behaviour is the need identification and looking for solution for the satisfaction of the need. The focus of rural marketers/producers is to identify and find out the needs of the urban consumers and to find out

the ways by which the rural products can be effectively offered to the consumers for the satisfaction of their needs. There are many products that the urban consumers are willing to purchase but they are not aware about the sources from where the products can be bought.

2. **Information Search**: The second step relates to the search for information for the satisfaction of the stated needs. This step refers to the process of getting all the information about the product. It is a stage in which a consumer searches for internal or external information. This process is same for the urban consumers as well for the rural consumers. The consumers need information about appropriate evaluative criteria, existence of alternatives and performance of each alternative on evaluative criterion.

Various sources of information search are as follows and includes:

- Personal sources: family members, friends, and reference groups.
- Commercial sources: Advertisements, Salespersons, promotional hoardings etc.
- Public Sources: Mass media and
- Self-Experiments like handling the product, using samples of products like shampoo sachets etc.

3. **Evaluation of Alternatives**: This step focuses on the various alternatives available to the customer for the satisfaction of needs. In this stage, consumers evaluate all the product and brand options on attributes which have the ability to deliver the benefit that the customer is seeking. The products that consumers compare form their evoked set which is also called as consideration set and it represent the alternatives being considered by consumers during the problem-solving process. For example in the purchase of a Carpet the decision criteria could be identified as follows:

- Price
- Design
- Support in terms of services and logistics.
- Repairs
- Warranties
- Reliability
- Multiple uses

4. **Purchase Decision**: This is the stage when the consumers make up their mind to make the particular purchase. During this time, the consumer forms an intention to buy the brand because he has evaluated all the alternatives and identified the value that it will bring him. The purchase decision is also affected by the availability of products at a particular point of time and changing nature of needs. When a desired need is not fulfilled an alternate goal emerges. Since the consumer has rational and emotional motivations, which are purely objective or subjective. Therefore Goal substitution occurs on non-attainment of the desired goal. The final purchase decision can be disrupted by two factors which are negative feedback and unanticipated situations like loss of job or closing down of retail store etc.

5. **Post-Purchase Behaviour**: The last stage of the consumer buying behaviour is the Post purchase behaviour which takes place after the product has been purchased. It is a general tendency of the customer to be satisfied or dissatisfied after the product purchase. The post purchase behaviour is based upon the consumer's own satisfaction arising due to his preference for a more profitable option of the available alternatives. The analysis of the psychological factors on the customer is done by the marketer to understand the reasons for their purchases and post purchase behaviour. Some companies now days engage with their consumers with post- purchase communications in order to influence their feelings about their post purchases. Methods like offering money back guarantees also enrich post-purchase communications between the company and its consumers.

Various factors those affecting the buying behavior of consumers are:

1. Environmental factors.
2. Geographic Factors.
3. Occupational factors
4. Place of purchase.
5. Innovations in the product in terms of usage and frequency.
6. Brand loyalty and Brand Equity.

In addition to the above factors there are some Cultural factors which influence the buying behaviour of consumer. The marketer has to give special focus and understanding to the role of culture in consumer buying behaviour. Culture is the first and basic element which has a substantial impact on the buying behaviour of the consumer. It shapes a person's needs, wants, demands and behaviour. In a diverse country like India there are so many different cultures, which make the job of a marketer very tough.

Some of the prominent cultural factors that have an influence on the consumer buying behaviour are as follows:

1. Product (colour, size, design, and shape).
2. Social rituals and practices.
3. The Decision-making process in the family.

Types of buying Behaviour

Complex Buying Behavior occurs when the consumer is highly involved with the purchase and there are significant differences between brands. In this type of buying behaviour the Consumers purchase those types of products which are costly and many times are one time purchases therefore the consumer invests considerable time and effort in purchasing the product. The consumers indulge in complex buying behavior when they are highly involved in the purchase process and are aware of significant differences among brands. Since the products are costly and expensive these products are bought infrequently and with much more deliberations. The purchase of these products is risky and highly self- expressive. For e.g. automobile, two-wheeler, house, high end jewellery etc.

Dissonance-Reducing Buying Behavior – The dissonance means dissatisfaction form the purchase of product which crops up after the purchase of the product. Sometimes the consumer is highly involved in the purchase of the high end product due to the limited differences between the brands the differentiation becomes difficult. The high involvement products are expensive, infrequent and risky. 'Dissonance' can occur if consumers worry afterwards that they may have made the wrong choice.

Habitual Buying Behavior – Habitual Buying Behavior refers to situations where a consumer has low involvement in a purchase, and perceives very few differences between products in a given product category. There are many products which fall in this category of routine purchases. These types of products are frequently purchased and less risky. These are low involvement products and less deliberations and time is given for the purchase of these products. Hence they are bought under conditions of low consumer involvement and the absence of significant brand differences. Most of them are everyday use products and commodities, such as toilet paper, salt and black pepper, salt, Candies, Needles etc.

Variety-Seeking Buying Behavior – It is the buying tendency of those consumers in which the consumers do not have a high involvement with a product and there is a significant difference between brands. These types of consumers seek variety for no genuine reasons and soon become bored with products. In many cases especially the urban consumers looks for variety in the products. These products are also characterized by low consumer involvement but significant brand differences. The consumer may shift to the other brand due to the boredom or just because of simple wish to try another product for a different taste. Due to the number of options in front of consumers, variety-seeking buyer behavior consumers typically do a lot of brand switching, or the decision of a consumer to purchase a brand other than the one they have previously used or purchased.

	High involvement	Low involvement
Significant differences between brands	Complex buying behavior	Variety seeking buying behavior
Few differences between brands	Dissonance reducing buying behavior	Habitual buying behavior

Recent Market Scenario in India

In the recent market scenario there are three major factors that are pertinent for the Indian companies' growth in the international market. Some of the factors are as follows:

1. High cost of delivery and the transportation costs from farm to the markets eat away the profits of the producer.

2. India's transport costs are higher due to fragmented Supply Chain due to policies inhibiting investment, integration and competition in transport sector, storage and distributions.

3. As per the World Bank survey there exists a huge disparity in health, safety, and quality standards as required by foreign governments and buyers, especially from developed countries. It has to be seen when Indian companies will be making for such stringent quality standards demands otherwise the Indian companies will not be able to compete even in domestic market.

The World Bank report has proposed two major reforms to raise the farmers' incomes, lower retail prices and improve the international competitiveness of rural producers. These are:

1. Create an integrated and competitive domestic agriculture market.
2. Improve communication, transport, storage, distribution and agriculture support services.

The following are the Changing scenario in the twenty-first century for India which is due to the following reasons:

- Opening of country's economy
- Global competition
- Better quality products
- A large variety of same products
- Technology advanced products
- New and better channels of distribution
- New and innovative channels of advertising
- Well informed customers.
- Complaint redressal forums

Characteristics of Urban and Rural Markets:

S. No.	Features	Rural	Urban
1	Literacy	Low	High
2	Per capita Income	Low	High
3	Demand	Seasonal	Uniform
4	Sources of Information	Word of mouth	Any Media
5	Knowledge of the product	Not known	Known
6	Branding	Mostly no	Mostly Yes
7	Consumer Protections Available	Rarely	Easily Available
8	After Sales Service	Inadequate	Adequate
9	Timely delivery	Untimely	Timely
10	Communication Facilities	Poor	Excellent

3

Rural Marketing Strategies

Introduction

A marketing strategy of a business is the game plan of an organization for approaching its target market effectively. Marketing strategy is also used to target the prospective customer and converting them into loyal consumers for the brand and services being offered by the companies.

A marketing strategy is the building block of a marketing plan and consists of the value which the company wants to offer, its key message which the company wants to convey to the target market and other elements which are key in the area of marketing.

Hence, a marketing strategy is the coordinated and comprehensive plan prepared by the company for achieving its marketing objectives. An effective marketing strategy helps the company to use the available resources in the best possible way to achieve sustainable competitive advantage. Marketing strategy provides a blueprint to the organization for attaining the marketing objectives which is carried out after proper marketing research.

Marketing Planning?

Marketing planning is a process that allows to determine goals and develop marketing strategies and techniques to achieve these goals.

Marketing planning implies

- Analyzing the existing situation, information and marketing opportunities
- Forecast and start planning
- Selecting target market(s)
- Defining marketing objectives
- Designing and developing a marketing strategy
- Allocating resources to achieve these objectives

For example, a company repositioning or rebranding requires more strategy and techniques to improve the new brand's visibility. A company that is in the launching phase, on the other hand, needs to focus on developing a go-to-market strategy

Types of marketing planning

There are two types of marketing planning:

- **Long-term marketing planning:** Long-term marketing planning is marketing planning for more than one year. It is the top management›s responsibility. This marketing planning sets future objectives and strategies, and it prepares a framework in which short-term plans are created. Long-term marketing planning includes, for instance, the selection of a price policy, a distribution channel and media advertising.
- **Short-term marketing planning:** Short-term marketing planning is marketing planning for less than a year, like bi-annual or annual plans. It is the responsibility of the mid-management. The short-term plans help to solve recurring issues.

Rural Marketing Strategies

The Indian market offers immense opportunities to foreign players. As the disposable income of Indian consumers is growing, more and more companies are entering the Indian markets with their innovative and multi-featured products. Due to the increased competition in the market every company is making marketing strategies that suit the Indian market. In this scenario the rural markets also have immense potential to offer a variety of products that can be produced by the rural producers and which would satisfy the needs of both urban and rural consumers. If these products are effectively marketed, then it can bear maximum profits to the rural producers and bigger revenues for the country. India's vast rural market offers a huge potential for a marketer facing stiff competition in the urban markets. The rural market environment is very different from the urban market and in recent times the rural markets in India have grown in size, range and sophistication.

- **A Model of Rural Marketing**
  - Acceptability
  - Affordability
  - Availability
  - Awareness

The 4 A's marketing concept states that these four elements are mandatory for the success of a product that can offer value to customers, society, as well as businesses.

Components of 4 A's Marketing Model

Acceptability

Acceptability means how much or to what extent does a product or service meets the expectations of the customers in a given market/niche. Are the customers satisfied? Did it fulfill their expectations or not? Sometimes, a product may even exceed the customers' expectorations. Acceptability is further categorized into two dimensions.

Types of Acceptability- 4 A's of Marketing

Functional Acceptability

Functional acceptability addresses the objective traits of a given product or service. It may include the performance, features, or facts about the product. For example, were the customers expecting these features? Are they actually useful for them even if they were not expecting them? Most importantly, will these features make the product more distinctive and attractive?

If a company makes a bigger cereal box to give "more" in "less," it seems a wonderful idea. However, if the box is too big to fit in the regular cupboard shelves, it will be placed somewhere else where it might be out of the customer's sight, thus ignored.

Psychological Acceptability

Psychological acceptability addresses the "subjective" traits of any product/ service that are perceived differently by the customers. Psychological acceptability describes how a customer perceives a product or brand from a societal point of view.

Companies like Rolls Royce, Mercedes, and BMW are luxury cars brands. They are generally regarded as a symbol of "eliteness" because it is not easy to own and maintain luxury cars from these companies. People take pride in using products from these brands.

Affordability

Affordability means the willingness and ability of a customer to pay for a certain product or service. Again, affordability has two further dimensions psychological and economic.

Types of Affordability In 4 A's of Marketing

Psychological Affordability

Psychological affordability refers to the willingness of a customer to pay for a particular product or service. That is, a customer is in a position to make the purchase but is he/she willing to do it? This depends on how the customer perceives that specific product. Will that product make him feel good? Or will it have any impact on his/her societal acceptance or even a source of appreciation or acceptance?

For example, oil field workers may prefer to drive Chevy Bolt or Nissan LEAF just because their peers drive tricked-out trucks.

Economical Affordability

Economic affordability refers to a customer's financial ability to buy a specific product. Does the customer you are targeting have enough financial resources to buy your product? For example, a customer may want to buy a product of HSN or QVC but is unable to do that unless these brands start offering a six-easy-payments method.

Affordability is important because it is helpful for businesses to create a product or service that is not only valuable but is cost-effective as well. Besides, affordability is more important when you develop your marketing campaign on reliability and cost-effectiveness.

Accessibility

Accessibility in 4 A's of marketing means the level of ease with which a product or service is accessible for the customers. Accessibility here basically addresses customer convenience and customer accessibility. Here are two further dimensions of accessibility

Types of Accessibility In 4 A's of Marketing

Customer Convenience

Customer convenience means how easy it is for a customer to obtain or get a product or service. Human psychology is pretty simple; customers always prefer the most accessible options. "An arm's length of desire" is exactly what Coca-Cola's former chairman said while explaining the importance of making the product readily available to the potential customer.

7- Eleven is really a perfect example of customer convenience. The company has established thousands of stores just to make sure that they are easily recognized and available to the customers.

Customer Availability

Availability here means whether the specific company has enough stock of a product to meet customers/market demand. If a customer wants a product at any given time while the company is out of stock, it will lead to customer dissatisfaction and force them to look for alternatives.

Awareness

Awareness basically addresses both existing and potential customers of a product or service. It focuses on things like;

- Informing customers/ and potential customers about the benefits and features of a product
- Persuading potential customers to make the purchase, and
- Maintaining a trustable relation with the existing customers.

Types of Awareness in 4 A's of Marketing

Product Knowledge

The customers must have sufficient knowledge about the product. The business must be able to inform its potential customers that they are selling this specific product or service. For example, Eliquis is a pharmaceutical drug that is used for the treatment of A-Fib. However, a massive number of patients only know about Warfarin or Xarelto because they don't have enough knowledge about Eliquis.

Brand Awareness

Brand awareness is a simple marketing term that defines how much customers remember, recall, or recognize a brand. For example, PepsiCo offers multiple products such a Pepsi-Cola, Mountain Dew, Frito-Lays, etc. But a customer may remember all these products just by hearing the word "Pepsi." Brand awareness is what actually differentiates a company from its competitors.

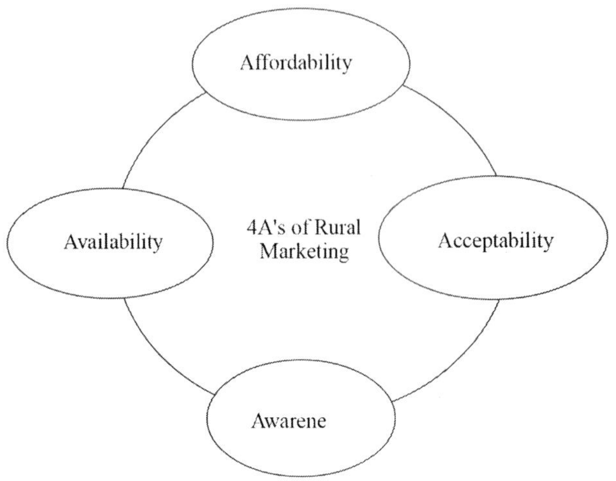

Fig. 2.1: 4A's of Rural Marketing

Source: Sarkar, D. N., & Pareek, G. (2013)

The 4A's of marketing explains that the product should be affordable to the target market that is the pricing should not be too high and not too low which may affect the price- sensitive consumers. Availability refers to regular supply of the product to the target market. Acceptability means that the product meets the required need of the consumer and it makes the consumer satisfied and finally Awareness means the use of communication mediums with which the consumers are made aware of the product and its benefits. For example the availability of sachets of shampoos and Lifebuoy small sized soaps and companies like ITC, HUL, P&G have used the communication effectively to make the consumer aware about their offerings.

Along with the 4A's of rural marketing the 4P's of marketing also plays an important in marketing strategy formulation. In fact, the 4A's revolves around the 4P's which is also referred to as Marketing Mix. The 4A's and P's should work in close coordination with each other. The marketing strategy of any company revolves around these 4P's and 4A's. The 4P's were given by Jerome McCarthy. The main elements of the marketing mix are given in the figure given below:

Fig. 2.2: The Rural marketing strategies
Source: McCarthy, E. J., (1979)

Marketing Mix (4 P's of Marketing)

The marketing mix, also known as the four P's of marketing, refers to the four key elements of a marketing strategy: product, price, place and promotion. By paying attention to the following four components of the marketing mix, a business can maximize its chances of a product being recognized and bought by customers:

- Product. The item or service being sold must satisfy a consumer's need or desire.
- Price. An item should be sold at the right price for consumer expectations, neither too low nor too high.
- Promotion. The public needs to be informed about the product and its features to understand how it fills their needs or desires.
- Place. The location where the product can be purchased is important for optimizing sales.

Understanding the 4 P's: Examples and considerations

The four P's are linked and work together. While various marketing concepts have been developed over time, the four P's are the basis for every successful marketing strategy. The following is a breakdown of each P with examples.

Product

Products are commodities and services that solve problems and satisfy the needs of consumers. A product can be tangible, such as a vehicle or a piece of clothing, or intangible, such as a cruise or house cleaning service. A successful product either fills a void in the marketplace or offers a unique experience that spikes demand.

Example. Before the iPhone was launched, most consumers did not realize the need for a phone that would let them access everything at their fingertips. The way Apple marketed its product compelled people to simplify their lives by carrying a smartphone that could also serve as a GPS, calendar, search engine, flashlight, weather guide and calculator.

Questions to ask. Before marketing a product, it is important to understand it intimately. This includes discovering details about the target audience and its preferences.

The following are some questions to answer before developing a product:

- What is the product?
- Is it a specific product or a service?
- What does the product accomplish?
- Does the product fulfill a need or provide a unique experience?
- Who are the target customers for the product?
- What differentiates the product from the competition?

The marketing mix consists of the four key elements of a marketing strategy: product, price, place and promotion.

Price

Price is the cost of the product that the consumer pays. During product marketing, it is important to set a price that reflects the current market trends and is affordable for consumers, yet at the same time is profitable for the business. Price can fluctuate based on the supply and demand and the product's sales cycle. While some businesses might lower the price to compete with the market, others might inflate it -- especially if they are promoting a luxury brand.

Example. Price points play a vital role in making a product successful. For example, if a product is overpriced, only a few consumers will purchase it. Conversely, a product that is priced too low can give consumers an impression of inferior quality, thus preventing them from purchasing it.

Questions to ask. To determine the most profitable price for a product, it is important to study the target audience and what they are willing to pay for that product.

The following are some questions to answer before establishing a product pricing strategy:

- How much do the competitors charge for similar products?
- What is the affordability and price range of target consumers?
- What is the lowest price that the product can sell for?
- What is the highest price that the product can sell for?
- What price is too high or too low for the target audience?
- What price is the best fit for the target market?

Place

This is where and how the product or service is purchased by the customers. It also entails where the product is stored and manufactured. Digital transformation has evolved how products are sold -- online, small local shops or global producers. This marketing plan also considers where the product is advertised and in which format, such as magazines, online ads, radio, infomercials or film product placements.

Example. The place is where the product is marketed and distributed from. For example, when targeting a product to seniors, it would be wise to not market it on TikTok. Similarly, products targeting the younger generations would gain more attention if they were promoted online and on social media platforms.

Questions to ask. Not every place is suitable for marketing and distributing a product. As such, it is important to distribute products and meet customer needs in a place that is easily accessible.

The following are some questions to consider before deciding on a place to market a product:

- Which places or venues do buyers frequent for similar products and services?
- Where is the competition selling its products?
- What are the shopping habits of the target audience?
- Will the product placement and distribution require a sales team, the use of Salesforce or will it be self-service?
- How can the right distribution channels be accessed?

Promotion

Promotion refers to reaching the target audience with the right message at the right time. It gets the word out and is an effective way to conduct a sales promotion and connect with consumers. A promotional strategy aims to show consumers why they would need a certain product and the reasons for buying it over other products. The core of marketing communications, product promotions push out specific and meaningful advertising through popular channels: word-of-mouth seeding, social networking, Instagram campaigns, print marketing, television commercials, email marketing campaigns, social media marketing and more.

Example. Timing can play an influential role in promotional marketing. Take, for example, the football season during which pizza delivery deals are targeted during games. This entices consumers to try new products they may not have enjoyed otherwise.

Questions to ask. For a product to be successful, setting the best price or being a great product offering is not enough. Promotion is the main ingredient in the marketing mix that can distribute the product to the masses. Therefore, the promotional messages should always cater to the target audience as well as to the distribution channels.

The following are some questions to consider when thinking about a promotional strategy:

- When is the right time to reach the target audience?
- Which channels or mediums will the target audience get their information from?
- What advertising approaches will be the most fruitful for the target audience?
- Which channels are the most cost-effective and efficient for product promotion?
- Which part of the target audience should be engaged?
- Where are the competitors spending their advertising efforts and marketing revenue?

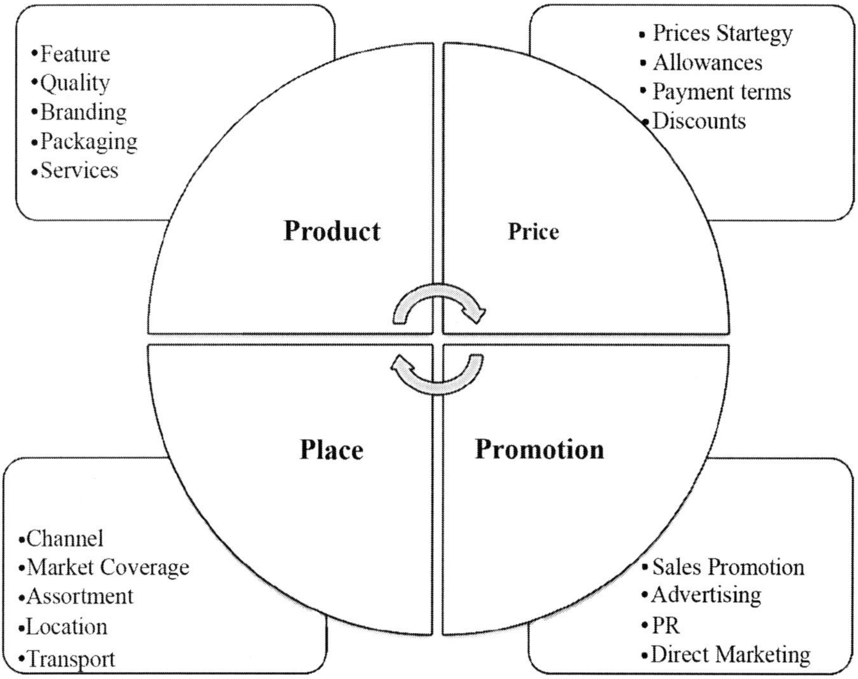

Fig. 2.3: The Marketing Mix

Source: McCarthy, 1960

Tangible and Intangible Rural Products

A product of an offering can be classified into two broad categories called as tangible and intangible products.

A tangible product is one that can be touched and felt. Tangible goods are products that you can put your hands on. As long as something is shipping to the consumer it will be a tangible good. Most of the goods in the market are tangible products. For example: Laptop, Tractor, Agricultural equipment, etc.

Whereas, an intangible product is a product that can only be perceived. Things like domain names or computer programs are intangible goods. The service sector is predominantly focused on the intangibility of the product only. For example Teaching, Consultancy, Airlines, Tourism, Medical Services are all part of services since they are intangible in nature. They are the goods that do not have a physical nature. Most of the services industry offers intangible products. In an increasingly digitized world; intangible goods play an important role in the economy of a country. Some of the examples of intangible products are Consultancy, Education, and Hotel industry. Intangible data products can further be classified into two categories which are virtual digital goods and real digital goods. Real digital goods are commonly viewed as 3-D objects or virtual transfer within the same visual media program for Traders Middlemen and labourers.

Some of the main differences between tangible and intangible goods are as follows:

Differences between tangible and intangible goods

Tangible Products	**Intangible Products**
A customer can see, feel, touch or taste the productbefore purchasing.	A customer cannot see, feel, touch or taste the product before purchasing. The benefits can onlybe imagined.
There is control over quality and consistency	The producer has less control over quality andconsistency.
The tangibles can be inventoried	The intangibles cannot be inventoried as they areperishable.

Analysing Marketing Strategies

Marketing strategies are generally based on explicit and implicit beliefs about the behavior of the consumers. The marketing Decisions based on explicit assumptions and sound theoretical and practical aspects are more likely to be successful as compared to the marketing decisions based solely on implicit intuition. The sound consumer behaviour knowledge can be an important tool for gaining competitive advantage while formulating the marketing strategies. It would be helpful in handling the risks and uncertainties of the marketing environment effectively. It can also reduce substantially the odds of bad decisions and market failures.

Some of the principles related to consumer behaviour which are kept under consideration by the marketers for effective formulation of marketing strategies are as follows:

• Analyzing Market Opportunity

Consumer behavior helps in identifying the unfulfilled needs and wants of the consumers. This requires scanning of the marketing environment and identification of the trends operating in the market area, like customer's lifestyles, income levels and technological advancements in the market.

Selecting Target Market

The scanning and evaluation of market opportunities helps in identifying different consumer segments with varying wants and needs. Identification of the target market and understanding the buying behaviour of the target market helps the marketer to design products and services as per the requirements of the target market.

Marketing-Mix Decisions with Examples

The marketing mixes are used and modified accordingly to formulate the marketing strategies. Once the needs, wants are identified, the marketer has then to strategise the precise marketing mix of four P's, i.e., Product, Price, Place, and Promotion. The different products lines of the company have different marketing mixes. Each variable of the marketing mix has to be modified as per the requirement of the market and the consumer.

Product

A product is the main thing with in which marketer design products or services accordingly to satisfy the needs or wants of consumers. Decisions related to the product are Quality, size, shape, variety and features. The marketer also decides about packaging, service aspects, warranties, credit facilities, and accessories.

Example – Nestle introduced Maggi noodles in masala and capsicum flavors. Subsequently, keeping in mind the consumer preferences of other regions of India, the company introduced other flavours which were popular in different regions of India, Garlic, Sambar, Atta Maggi, Soupy noodles, cuppa noodles, spicy vegetables noodles.

Price

The price should commensurate with the quality of the product. There are different pricing strategies like penetration, skimming and psychological etc which can be used by the companies in pricing the product. Marketers must decide what price to be charged for a product or service, to stay competitive in the market. In many cases the companies tries to emulate the pricing strategies of the competitors.

Place

The place component of the marketing mix is related to the distribution channel and supply chin activities of the company i.e., where and how to offer the products and services at the final stage. The main decisions taken regarding the distribution mix are as follows:

- Should the different products categories be sold through different retail outlets or only through the selected ones?
- Should the marketer focus on the outlets that sell the competing brands? Or, should they focus on elite outlets selling the marketer's brands only?
- The location of the retail outlets keeping customers' point of view?
- Should the company go for direct marketing and selling?

Promotion

Promotion is used in the marketing strategies to build long term mutually beneficial relationship with the consumers through the integrated marketing communication. In the Promotion mix as already discussed the marketer has to decide which method would be most suitable to effectively reach the consumers. Should it be advertising alone or should it be combined with sales promotion techniques? The company has to focus on its target consumers, their location, and preferences, which media have, better accessibility for target consumers, the lifestyles of the consumers, etc.

Therefore understanding of the consumer behaviour is an important aspect of the marketing strategy. Without the proper understanding of the consumer behaviour it would become very difficult for the marketer to effectively formulate the strategies. The marketer also focuses on the buying patterns of the consumer which consists of the when, why and where of the buying process and under what conditions the product is consumed. Since the urban consumer is more informed due to exposure to the external environment therefore the buying behaviour of the urban consumers is different as compared to the rural consumers. Due to better infrastructure and other factors like high income levels, high literacy rate and with high disposable income the propensity to adopt a value offering product becomes high. Therefore the marketers should formulate the marketing strategies which are especially catering to the urban and rural consumers.

Complex Buying Behavior occurs when the consumer is highly involved with the purchase and there are significant differences between brands. In this type of buying behaviour the Consumers purchase those types of products which are costly and many times are one time purchases therefore the consumer invests considerable time and effort in purchasing the product. The consumers indulge in complex buying behavior when they are highly involved in the purchase process and are aware of significant differences among brands. Since the products are costly and expensive these products are bought infrequently and with much more deliberations. The purchase of these products are risky and highly self expressive. For e.g. automobile, two-wheeler, house, high end jewellery etc.

Dissonance-Reducing Buying Behavior

The dissonance means dissatisfaction form the purchase of product which crops up after the purchase of the product. Sometimes the consumer is highly involved in the purchase of the high end product due to the limited differences between the brands the differentiation becomes difficult. The high involvement products are expensive, infrequent and risky. 'Dissonance' can occur if consumers worry afterwards that they may have made the wrong choice. For example, carpet buying. In such a buying the consumer might experience dissonance that may be due to some disliking features of the carpet. Consumer will choose such products on the basis of price or convenience and seek confirmation, after the purchase, of their decision. Therefore to reduce the dissonance the marketing communication should focus on reducing the dissonance and making the consumer satisfied about the consumer's choice for his or her brand.

Habitual Buying Behavior – Habitual Buying Behavior refers to situations where a consumer has low involvement in a purchase, and perceives very few differences between products in a given product category. There are many products which fall in this category of routine purchases. These types of products are frequently purchased and less risky. These are low involvement products and less deliberations and time is given for the purchase of these products. Due to this products are bought under conditions of low consumer involvement and the absence of significant brand differences. Most of them are everyday use products and commodities, such as toilet paper, salt and black pepper, salt, Candies, Needles etc.

Variety-Seeking Buying Behavior

It is the buying tendency of those consumers in which the consumers do not have a high involvement with a product and there is a significant difference between brands. These types of consumers seek variety for no genuine reasons and soon become bored with products. In many cases especially the urban consumers looks for variety in the products .These products are also characterized by low consumer involvement but significant brand differences. The consumer may shift to the other brand due to the boredom or just because of simple wish to try another product for a different taste. Due to the number of options in front of consumers, variety-seeking buyer behavior consumers typically do a lot of brand switching, or the decision of a consumer to purchase a brand other than the one they have previously used or purchased. Since the cost to change potato chip brands is relatively low, then you might change brands strictly out of sheer boredom. The marketer tries to encourage habitual buying behavior of the consumers by dominating the shelf space, avoiding out of stock conditions, sponsoring frequent reminder advertising, offering lower prices, deals, coupons and free samples. Variety-seeking buyer behaviors in consumers can cause a major problem for marketers. The problem which all marketers wish to solve is that how they can fight consumers with these behaviors.

Marketing Communications

Communication refers to the transfer of information, ideas, thoughts between sender and the receiver. In order to make the communication process effective the barriers should be minimized and the ambiguity in the communication process should be avoided. Effective communication strategies can do wonders for the company. For Example Companies like Coca-Cola, Perfetti, Pepsi, Nestle and others have been able to effectively communicate the benefits of their product to their target market. Broadly there are two types of the communication process which are used by companies to promote their product. They are:

- Formal Communication
- Informal Communication

Formal communication is through organized channels which are set by the companies. The Channels are communicated by the top management in advance and conveyed to the lower-level employees. This communication flows through deliberately created official recognized channels to ensure a smooth, orderly, and timely flow of information. Some of the examples of formal communication are indictments, lawsuits, civil and criminal litigation, and court proceedings, Business correspondences etc.

Informal communication is through unorganized channels. It can take place anywhere within the organization. The main aim of informal communication is to establish close relationships. It is faster as compared to the formal communication process. Informal communication is critical to businesses because it encourages upward communication and facilitates communication between employees with their superiors. This leads to higher employee morale. Informal communication is an effective method for conflict resolution and increasing brand equity.

Role of Technological Developments

Technology has made the consumer more powerful and with the internet enabled smart phone and tablets the convenience offered by technology has transformed the way shopping was done. Technological factors take in to consideration the existence, availability, and development of technology. The expansion of the telecommunication and other communication networks has provided immense opportunities to the marketers to use this for their advantage in the rural as well as urban markets, and also to be in constant with their target market. Development of cable and digital networks has made the usage of Television very effective in passing on the message related to products and services to the rural and urban consumers. In the urban areas the youths and children have access to information regarding the performance and usage of the product. Information technology and internet have the capacity to spread up information in urban India as jungle fire. The recent initiatives of the central government under its Digital India programme, the government intends to transform the India's rural economy by creating skilled jobs in rural areas so that the rural people can become job providers than job seekers.

To conclude the technological factors are the important factors that can affect the rural businesses. There is no doubt that technology has changed the way the companies used to conduct their business. It's difficult to believe that in the past ten years the significance of so many things has changed almost so fast. Some of the examples of Technological Factors which affect the business are as follows:

- 3 Dimensional technology
- Computer calculation speed/power
- Engine efficiency
- Internet connectivity
- Wireless charging
- Automation
- Security
- Augmented Reality
- Mobile devices and Payments
- Social media
- Integration of technologies like IOT, Big data and cloud Technology

These above technologies have proved to influence consumer buying behaviour intention positively. The technological factors have favorably changed the customer's shopping behavior. The companies by the use of latest technologies have achieved positive outcomes and augmented product knowledge with a positive attitude towards the brand leading to higher purchase intentions.

• Rural Marketing Environment

Economic Factors

The Consumer behaviour is largely influenced by the economic factors. The economic factors that influence consumer behaviour are:

- Personal Income
- Family income
- Income expectations
- Savings
- Liquid assets of the Consumer
- Consumer credit
- Other economic factors.

Economic factors are an indispensable factor for sustainable development of the rural economy. The economic factors have the potential to uplift the rural population out of poverty. A large rural population still depends on low-productivity farming for their livelihoods. The rural households lack access to business opportunities and marketing support of their products and therefore the rural population and often rely on income from wage employment. The mitigation of extreme poverty in rural areas in India requires government attention and initiatives in terms of increased policy focus on rural development. Work in the rural economy on national and international policy agendas is crucial to find long-term solutions to the problems responsible for contributing in the rural poverty. The major factors which contributes to the rural poverty are weak institutions, ineffective law enforcement and compliance; non availability of enabling environment for businesses; underdeveloped production systems; poor infrastructure and limited access to services, finance and health-care. Close coordination between all government departments and rural stakeholders is essential for ensuring better result with high impact. The productive transformation of both agriculture and non-agricultural economy cannot be effectively achieved without the active involvement of government and rural stakeholders. Improving the quality of agricultural jobs and providing business opportunities and marketing support is essential to attract rural youth. This can facilitate agricultural growth, which will raise rural incomes, and will have multiplier effects. The rise in global food demand, the agricultural sector offers untapped employment opportunities. To attract the new generation, the sector needs modernization, to increase its dynamism and to raise its status as a source of business opportunity. Rural areas have great diversity of economic activities, which includes processing and marketing of agricultural products, tourism, mining and services. Harnessing the potential of the rural economy is the need of the hour which represents a purpose that has to learn from past experiences and develop new strategies for the future.

Marketing Environment

The Indian marketing environment consists of a diverse population having different cultures, different languages. Some of the consumers in India are informed consumers who have disposable incomes to fulfill their needs with a branded product, whereas some are illiterate with low incomes. This diversity of the Indian market offers various challenges to the marketers which need to be tackled differently for various market segments. A marketing environment consists of various tangible and intangible factors, which can be controllable or uncontrollable. Marketing strategy is using the marketing mix to tailor - make the marketing strategies for the targeted market of an organization. The marketing environment also includes threats and opportunities in the market. The marketing environment of India is very complex and is fast changing due to technological innovations. The marketing organization should be proactive and adopt strategies according to the changing requirements of the market. A Company has to be in sync with time to withstand competition. An organization that makes effective and creative marketing strategies prospers and creates opportunities in the changing environment. There are various factors which constitutes the marketing environment, they are:

a) Social changes which consist of three sub-factors as:

- Sociological factor
- Anthropological factors
- Psychological factors

b) Economic changes consist of factors like:

- Competition
- Consumers
- Price

Other important change factors in the marketing environment are:

- Ethical changes
- Political changes
- Physical changes
- Technological changes

India has gone through many changes in the field of marketing and the most important have been the economic liberalization after 1991. The Indian consumers have become more informed, influential and have considerable disposable income due to the increase in sources of income. The Indian consumers have become more demanding and look for those products which were considered as luxuries earlier. This situation largely prevails in the urban India because this segment was given maximum attention after liberalization and globalization in 1991.The marketers of the new millennium have started to treat Indian market as one single entity rather than urban or rural markets. The companies have started investing in research and studies to enter in the markets with accurate information. Around 73 per cent of the Indian population live in 5, 72,000 vastly spread villages of India as per Indian census, 2011.The companies have started to acknowledge the potential of this market looking at the sheer numbers. The rural producer grows vegetables and with extensive milk distribution network many things comes naturally with to the rural marketers. Improvements in the field of agriculture, health, education, communication, electrification, etc. have improved the life of the rural population and market research agencies forecast that the rural demand will supersede the urban demand in the coming future.

Occupation Pattern

The occupational pattern of a segment naturally has an impact on the buying behavior of the consumers due to higher disposable income. A salaried person has an assured monthly income whereas a daily wage earner has a varied income. Their occupation and income affect their buying behavior also. As the maximum number of rural consumers has agriculture as the main occupation so therefore their income is seasonal and keeps varying which is not in the case of urban consumers.

Income Generation

The pattern of income generation in rural areas is varied and seasonal unlike the fixed monthly income in the urban areas. This created a consumption pattern that is quite different from the urban one. The major sources of income generation for rural consumers are as follows:

- By sale of agricultural produce
- By sale of animal products, For example, Milk, etc
- By interest on investment
- Government subsidies and grants
- By mortgage of properties and gold
- By charities and donations
- By labor and wages – Labourers do jobs in the construction of roads, bridges and buildings.

To conclude it can be surmised that the income of the Rural Sector is rising steadily because of the rural centric schemes of the government for job creation and entrepreneurship development The Percentage of Very Rich, Consuming Class, and Climbers are rising whereas Aspirants and Destitute are declining.

Literacy Level and Rural Demand

Due to the lower level of literacy in rural India the use of technology and other means of promotional tools become difficult. This is a challenge that the rural producers have to face as compared to the multinational companies. But due to the increase in the literacy levels of the rural population this weakness will soon be nonexistent and the rural producers will be able to use technology to promote their products. Also due to the governments, special schemes for girl education and the overall education of the rural consumers this situation is fast changing. As per the government data there is a rise of 23 % in the literacy level of rural consumers in the last 20 years. Due to an increase in literacy level the rural consumers are now able to make more informed choices and mature purchase decisions and have become more aware of the different brands and services available to them. The rural marketers, therefore, have to now make proper and effective marketing and communication strategies for urban consumers. The marketers have to use various communication tools and media for conveying the message to the consumer effectively so that the rural demand can be increased. Now communication is not a problem as far as communicating with rural consumers is concerned. Internet, Mobile phones and television have proved to be an effective medium for communication with the rural masses. This phenomenon can show slight variations in some states although efforts are being made to bring these areas also in the ambit.

Innovation and Diffusion

Everett Rogers proposed different categories of adopters based around the premise that different consumers respond to innovation differently, and therefore they are thus placed in different consumer categories, which he classified as innovators, early adaptors, early majority, late majority, and laggards. The Diffusion of innovation manifests itself in different ways in different societies and cultures and is dependent on the type of adopters and the innovation-decision process. The elaboration of each category of adopters is as given below:

Innovators

The customers who fall in the category of Innovators are those who are very enthusiastic about trying new things in the market. They are the ones who try to be the first ones in adopting the new innovations in the market. The innovators are the customers who love taking risks and they are adventurous in trying out new offerings, ideas, services and products. As already discussed They are risk takers, and do not fear trying out something new even if the innovative product does not provide the type of satisfaction as desired form the offering. The innovators do not care about the bad results in trying new products. The innovators are the most lucrative customers for any marketer and efforts should be made by the organization to reach out to these types of customers for marketing the new and innovative products.

Early Adopters

The early adopters are those who act as the opinion leaders in the markets. They act as reference groups for many customers and enjoy leadership roles. They are relatively flexible to adopt innovative offerings. The early adopters are ready for change and they are in look out for innovative and contemporary products for progressive changes in the environment. This type of adopters offers an attractive market and the marketer should appeal to this population by using marketing tools and other methods which may include detailed 'how-to' manuals and information sheets on implementation. Aggressive selling and marketing efforts are not required for this type of adopters and hence they don't need to be perused too much to purchase innovative products as they themselves are more than eager for change and trying out new products. Early adopters are described as curious and exploratory consumers, who buy first, talk fast and help in diffusion of the innovative products they also talk about the pros and cons of what they have purchased.

Early Majority

This category of customers lacks leadership qualities, but they adopt innovative products, ideas and services before the average person. They observe and analyze the market before going for actual purchase; they are calm and patient by nature. They satisfy themselves and wait till they are convinced about the innovation. They look for evidence before they purchase or adopt an innovative product. Various strategies which are available for the marketer to convince and target this category include Success stories of the innovations and verification of the innovation's effectiveness. These peoples look for dependable evidences before going for actual purchase.

Late Majority

This category of customers are resistant to change, they are satisfied with the existent products, they are skeptical of change. These types of customers are the ones who adopts the innovation only when therefore is a positive feedback about the innovation and the product has been tried by the majority of

the market. They look for empirical evidences to gauge the satisfaction level of customers who have tried the product and are happy with it. The various strategies which can be used to appeal to this category of adopters include information on how many other people have tried the innovation and have adopted it successfully with empirical proof.

Laggards

These types of customers are very conservative and are bound by tradition. They are very rigid and are the most difficult group to please. They don't want to change because of reasons which are personal to them. This type of consumers has to be convinced or confused for making them adopt the innovative products. The other Strategies which can be used to appeal to this population may include fear appeals, and pressure from people in the reference or peer groups. So it can be concluded form above that in the market place can find different types of adopters, As per the data from Lean Monitor their study found out that almost 34 percent of the consumers in the market are the early and late majority consumers and they have a substantial numbers in the marketplace. The category of Laggards makes up 16% of the consumer profile, whereas early adopters (13.5%) and innovators (2.5%).Thus this statistics by lean monitor is an indicator that how important it is to get the early customer awareness phase's right. In the end it can be concluded that diffusion of Innovations is a theory of how, why, and at what rate new ideas and technology spread through cultures.

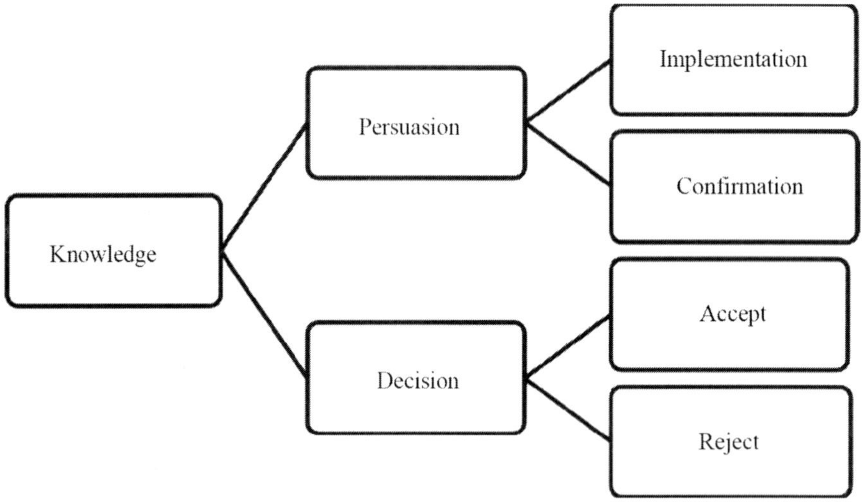

Fig. 2.4: Stages in Decision making process

Source: Rogers (2003)

Five Adoption Factors

Everett Rogers described some intrinsic characteristics of innovation that acts as a strong influence in an individual's decision regarding the adoption or rejection of an innovation. Some of the intrinsic characteristics are given as below:

1. **Relative Advantage**: This intrinsic advantage confirms how improved the innovation is over the previous product. What are the benefits which the new product is offering which were not being offered by the earlier product?
2. **Compatibility**: The compatibility means the emotional connect with the product. The higher the level of compatibility the better the innovation will be assimilated into a customer's life.
3. **Complexity or Simplicity**: The innovations no matter how advanced should be simple to use. The innovations which are too complicated or difficult to use are less likely to be adopted by the consumer.
4. **Trialability**: How easily an innovation may be tried is an important characteristic which decides whether the innovation will be adopted or not. If a consumer is able to try and test an innovation, then it is more likely that the innovation would be adopted.

5. **Observability**: Observability refers to the extent that an innovation is visible to others. An innovation that is more visible to the consumers will drive communication among the individual's peers and personal networks, which in turn will create more positive or negative reactions about the innovations.

Elements of Diffusion of Innovations

Some of the elements of Diffusion of Innovation are:

1. **Innovation**: As per Everett Rogers innovation is an idea, practice, or object that is perceived as new by the consumer. It is another unit on adoption. The adoption requires time and effort.
2. **Communication Channels**: A communication channel is "the means by which messages are sent from one prospect to another. An effective communication channel converts prospect into consumer.
3. **Time**: The innovation-decision time is the length of time required to pass through the innovation decision process. Rate of adoption is the speed with which an innovation is adopted by the consumers.
4. **Social System**: A social system is the environment in which the customer interacts with the marketers. It is defined as a set of interrelated units that are engaged in solving of the problem or need fulfillment of the customer to achieve a common goal.

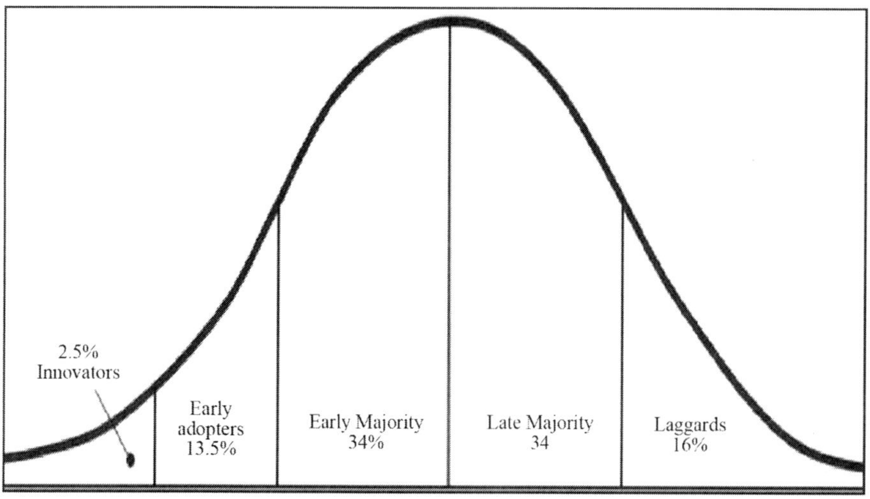

Fig. 2.5: Diffusion of Innovation

Source: Rogers and Everett (1962)

Opinion Leaders

The opinion leaders are those whose advice the consumer takes for making any purchase decisions. The consumers often take advice from those peoples who have already used the product and know about the product. The opinion is generally an educated person, who has knowledge about the product and its market. The opinion leader can be trusted for correct opinion on the Subject. In rural India the Sarpanch or Pradhan is usually considered to be the opinion leader, whereas in the urban India the opinion leaders are educated people. The Opinion-leaders are mostly product specific. The opinion of the leader varies from products to product. The more aware consumer takes second or even third opinion until they are satisfied. The marketers extend the theory of opinion leadership in advertising by using the brand ambassadors as product endorsers. It is always beneficial for the marketer to have a good understanding of the consumer buying behaviour in order to guide decisions in the urban or rural markets. In the present scenario the consumers can afford high priced brands and the rural consumers not only can afford the high process but are also willing to buy high priced brands.

Brand Loyalty

Brand loyalty is defined as positive feelings towards a brand and commitment and motivation to go for repeat purchase regardless of a competitor's offering the same product. Positive word of mouth is an important element of brand loyalty. Brand loyalty increases the brand equity of the company. Brand loyalty helps in creating an emotional connect with the brand. The urban consumers are more in to brand loyalty which means that they will go for the repeat purchase if the brand gives reasonable satisfaction. The entry for new brands in urban markets are possible, even though the urban market is considered to be a highly brand loyal market, this makes the urban market lucrative for the rural products. The Brand loyalty is low in case of FMCG products like toilet soaps, toothpaste, batteries etc. but it is high for the products like Soft drinks, and beauty creams, Shampoos etc. In a monopolistic market the Brand loyalty is possibly low because of the absence of variety of products. It is a good measure for the marketers to predict brand performance outcomes. Brand loyalty highlights the importance of integrated marketing communication in promoting a certain product. Brand loyalty is different from repurchasing as repurchasing may be due to situational constraints whereas brand loyalty is the motivation to purchase the product again and again. A strong brand loyalty indicates that the customers are willing to pay higher prices for the product. From the marketer's point of view, brand loyalty is a key factor and the companies often ensure that they are not wasting resources to retain loyal but unprofitable customers.

Status of Loyalty

The brand loyalty varies from consumer to consumer. Philip Kotler defines four status of loyalty. They are as follows:

1. Hard-core Loyals – They are the consumers who always purchase the same brand all the time. For Example: Heavy Smokers,
2. Split Loyals – These are the consumers who are loyal to two or three brands in case of non availability of the preferred brand they shift to the other brand. For Example if some consumer does not get coke it can purchase Pepsi or Thumbs up.
3. Shifting Loyals – These types of consumers keeps shifting from one brand to another. They are variety seekers and not satisfied with the one brand. This normally happens with the low involvement products. For Example: Stationary items like pen, pencil etc.
4. Switchers – These types of consumers have no loyalty towards particular brand. For Example Unbranded products.

Factors Influencing Brand Loyalty

There are many factors which influences the Brand Loyalty of consumers towards the product. The loyalty towards a brand is determined by varied psychological processes. The important factors which influence the brand loyalty of a customer towards a brand are Customer perceived value, brand trust, customer satisfaction, repeat purchase behavior, and commitment. Commitment towards a brand is considered to be essential requirement for brand loyalty followed by perceived value, satisfaction, and brand trust.

Fred Reichheld, an eminent writer on the area of brand loyalty, suggested that enhancing loyalty of the customer towards the brand have a significant impact on the profitability of the company.

Therefore proper research is required before spending money on the CRM programs. The main benefit which is an outcome of brand loyalty is longer tenure of customer and lower sensitivity towards the price. Many researchers have indicated that brand loyal customers are less sensitive towards price increases, because it is difficult for them to completely stop using the brand.

Integrated marketing communications (IMC) which is integrating a variety of convincing messages can be used as a potent tool to increase brand loyalty and to increase perceived attraction between the consumer and the brand. IMC is used to boost emotional response and attachment to the brand, as well as to create an emotional connect with the brand this in turn leads to brand loyalty. IMC can be used to increase the brand image, brand awareness, brand equity, and to achieve the shared values between the consumer and the brand. Brand loyalty can also be achieved through loyalty programs which increases bond between a brand and a consumer.

4

Rural Distribution

Introduction

There are many distribution networks which an organization may use depending upon the nature and usage of the product. Generally, there are two types of distribution networks which are being widely used the first is direct selling to the customer and the second is to have intermediaries in between which ensures that the product is available to the final consumer. In this indirect method the company is not in direct touch with the customer and this gap is filled by the middleman. The middleman not only provides the product to the customer but he also provides continuous feedback to the organization about the product and market demands. In this method the producer of the product is behind the screen and is dependent on the middleman for any demand or feedback from the customer side. Here the middleman can also provide wrong information to the producer as well. Another disadvantage of having the intermediaries is that it inflates the price of the product due to which the benefits are not passed on to the final consumer. Therefore, to pass on the benefit to the final consumer it becomes important that the companies have an effective distribution system so that the consumer feels happy and satisfied with product at the reasonable price.

In the competitive market every company is trying to outdo other in the in making their product available to the final consumer, but to have a competitive advantage in the area of distribution it is important that the companies carry out innovations in their distribution methods. Since distribution is all about bridging the gaps between manufacturer and customers therefore this gap should be reduced to the minimum with effective distribution systems. Every element in the distribution network has its own requirements, and it works in a unique operating environment, which the companies must keep into account. With the introduction of latest technologies in the area of distribution networks the distribution system has undergone transformation which every company must incorporate in their distribution strategies. This unit discusses how the distribution networks decides the manner in which product would be made available to the final consumer. The design of physical distribution is known as logistics and supply chain management and trade channels which are the part of distribution networks are the major components in distribution strategies.

Concept and Nature of Distribution

Marketing Intermediaries in the Distribution Channel

The marketing intermediaries are an important constituent of the distribution channel. They are one who is instrumental in the movement of products and services from producers to the final consumers. The Marketing intermediaries are an important link between the company and the end consumer. The different categories of marketing intermediaries which are most prevalent in the distribution channel are as follows:

- **Agents**: Agents are generally the sales representatives of the producer or the wholesalers whereas they differ from the brokers in the sense that the broker brings buyers and sellers together on a common platform. The services of the agents and the brokers are usually taken on a commission basis by the buyer or seller. Agents and brokers are into making of profitable deals. They are the part of the distribution network which do not own or take possession of the finished goods.
- **Industrial Distributors**: It is different type of the intermediary in the sense that they are independent wholesalers that purchases product lines related to their expertise only from manufacturers and sell them to the industrial users. They are more into B2B type of transactions. They maintain a sales force to properly execute these transactions. They provide services like call on purchasing agents, deliveries, credit facilities, and providing information. The Industrial distributors are common in big industries like aircraft manufacturing, mining, and oil companies.
- **Wholesalers:** Wholesalers sell finished products to the retailers, manufacturers, and institutions. The concept of wholesaling is very old and their main function is to buy from manufacturers and sell to retailers.
- **Retailers:** Retailers are firms that sell goods to the final consumers and to industrial users for their personal consumption. The retailers provide the aesthetics and ambience which makes the purchase process convenient.

Functions of Distribution Channels

The distribution channels are not just a link between the producer and the consumer but they serve many other functions which are related to the marketing activities. Distribution channels provide ownership utility to the utility by making available the product as and when required by the consumer. They also provide time and place utility to the producer. Apart from the main function of making the products available the distribution channels also carry out the following functions, which are as follows:

- **Logistics and Physical Distribution**: The distribution Marketing channels are responsible for assembling and sorting of the product and the transportation of goods from producer to the end customers.
- **Facilitation**: Distribution Channels also provides pre-sale and post-purchase services for smooth accessibility of the product to the customer, the service which includes are credit facilities, easy and quick financing, services, providing timely information and channel communication and coordination.
- **Creating Efficiencies**: The distribution channels create efficiencies by breaking bulk and creating assortments. The Wholesalers purchase substantial amount of finished products from the producer and then break them in to small assortments and sell them further to different channels and customers. The distribution channels make available a variety of products at a single location so that the customers don't have to move from one location to other for purchasing the product. This is of huge benefit for the customer as it saves the time and money of the customer.
- **Risks Sharing:** The distribution channels purchases the products from the manufacturer in bulk beforehand and it becomes their responsibility to sell the products for the profits. They make all possible efforts to sell the products otherwise the products not sold poses a severe risk to the channel in terms of inventory carrying costs. Therefore, the distribution channels share the risks along with the manufacturer.
- **Marketing:** The Distribution channels are also known marketing channels because they are an important element in the marketing strategy formulation. As they are in direct contact with the customer they are instrumental in creating brand equity and brand awareness about the product in the market. They are an important source of getting feedback from the consumer and passing on the feedback to the producer for product upgradation.

Role, Significance and Importance of Distribution Channels

Distribution Channels plays an important role in the efficient distribution and marketing of the products. They have the requisite knowledge, network and expertise about the products which they are offering to the target market. Due to technological advancements the consumer preferences have undergone considerable changes and the companies are working to make their distribution systems effective so to meet the requirement of the consumer. The distribution channels are facing many challenges due to the changed market environment. In order to overcome these challenges, the distribution channels have to look ahead of the traditional methods. Some of the important role of the distribution channels has been discussed below:

- **Distribution Channels act as a Salesman**: The distribution channels play the role of a salesman by creating demands for new products in the market. They have the expertise and skills to effectively sell the product by positive word of mouth and other marketing tools. They provide pre and post purchase service to the customer. They are in regular contact with the customer and provide valuable feedback to the company and the customer in case of any modifications are required in the product.
- **Distribution Channels Enrich Distributional Efficiency**: The distribution channels make the transfer of goods and services from producer to the consumer smooth. Since they are in regular contact with the consumer they know the purchasing patterns and ease of access of the end consumer. They understand the gap and try to fill this gap between producer and the consumer. They try that the consumers get the product as and when it is required by him. In the present times when the customers are always in a hurry the customer can very easily switch to the competitor's product if he/she is not getting the product from the preferred supplier at a particular time. An effective distribution can help in reducing the inventory carrying cost and the transportation costs also.
- **Customized Assortments**: The distribution channels have the expertise in transporting the finished product to a large number of retailers. In turn the retailers have the expertise in product assortment so that the product can be given to the maximum number of customers. It is because of the distribution channel only that the consumer is able to get the right product at the right time. Thus, the distribution channels help in offering the customized assortments to the customers.
- **Product Presentation and Merchandising:** The distribution channels supplies the product to the retailer. The retail with the help of effective

presentation of the product and the aesthetics is able to market the product in an effective manner. This presentation of the merchandise facilitates the product movement from the retail store to the customer. The customer gets fascinated by the attractive display of the product, and is enticed to purchase the product. The presentation persuades the consumer to shift from a regular brand. Thus merchandising activities of the distribution channels act as silent salesman at a retail store.

- **The channels help in executing the price mechanism between the producer and the consumer**: The distribution channels helps in deciding a price which is acceptable to both the producers as well to the final consumers.
- **Distribution Channels Assist in Stock Holding:** The other important function of the distribution channel is to, store the inventory, bear the risks, provide financing and provide the required warehouse space.
- **Goods Availability:** The distribution channels with the help of the retailer ensure that the right kind of goods is given to the right retailer for the sorting purpose to meet consumer needs at the point of purchase.
- **Simplified Transactions:** To efficiently carryout routine and simplified transactions and work with a large number of products reasonable distribution cost and also to provide information to the sellers for formulating better business strategies.
- **Informed Choices:** The distribution channel helps the consumer in making informed choices and makes the right recommendations to their customers.

In view of the above it can be said that the distribution channels are an important element of the marketing strategy of the company. An effective distribution strategy is one of the important tasks for the company. The success and failure of the product depends on the distribution channels as it is the element which deals what, why, which and where of the production distribution which will provide revenue to the company. With growing business volumes and worldwide distribution prospects, distribution channels role is self-explanatory.

Need for Distribution / Distribution Channels

The Distribution channels are an important element of the marketing mix and they are required by the companies to provide right kind of products at the right time as and when required by the final consumer. When the marketing companies have large market to cater in such a situation it becomes difficult for the companies to reach each customer to offer the product. In such a situation the distributor plays a crucial role in supplying the products to the end consumer. The distributor plays an important role when the companies face resource, time or cost constraints. In such a case when the company is facing theses constraints the distribution channels with their expertise ensures the smooth distribution of products to maximum number of consumers. An effective distribution network ensures that the company gets the competitive advantage in the market through effective distribution networks.

Distribution Patterns for Consumer and Industrial Goods

In the present scenario where geographical boundaries do not play a major role the companies tries to sell their products nationally as well as internationally. This is possible only through an efficient distributor network. The size and the reach of the network depend on the geographical area which needs to be covered by the producer. The goods can broadly be divided in to two categories they are Industrial goods and consumer goods. Both the goods have different distribution networks because of the type of the product. The distribution channels followed for industrial and consumer goods are as shown below:

Industrial Goods

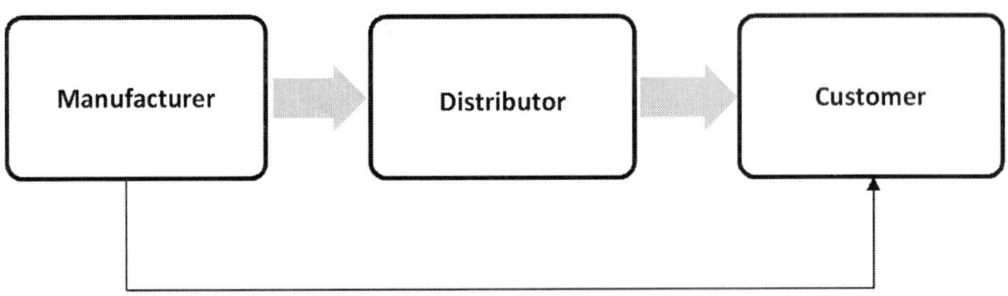

Fig. 3.1: Distribution channel for industrial goods (Mishra, 2008)

As shown in the figure, the industrial goods are directly sold to the customer with the help of a distributor. This is done due to the following reasons:

- Since the goods involved are complex in nature so the technicalities of the product have to be told to the customer, which can be best done by the manufacturer only.
- Since the industrial goods are expensive products so the companies don't want to share their profits with the intermediary. Moreover, the companies don't want to pass on the burden of price rise due to intermediary commission on the consumer.

- The Installation and commissioning of the machinery is appropriately done by the, company engineers. The after sales service is also given due consideration by the manufacturer only because of the nature of the product. The After-sales service is complicated in the case o industrial goods.

Consumer Goods

The other category of products which are referred to as consumer goods are sold through different type of distribution channels as shown below

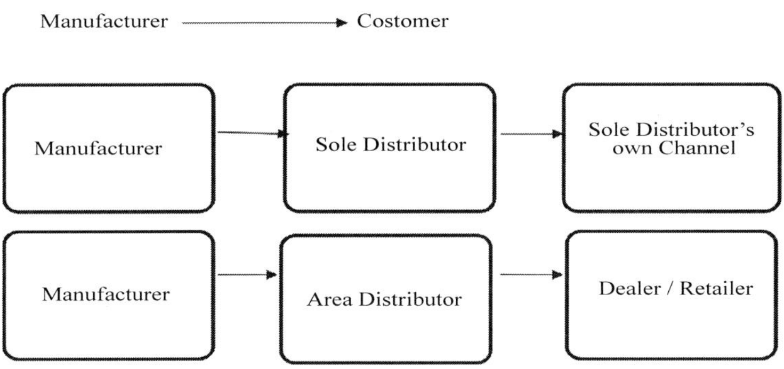

Fig. 3.2: Distribution channel for consumer goods (Mishra, 2008)

Small firms which have a small market share don't indulge in intermediaries in their distribution channels due to the costs involved and therefore try to reach the final consumer directly. Large firms which have a substantial market share to target and supply the product likes to involve the distributors because the company themselves cannot cater to the large market. The companies are able to approach the right consumer with the right product at the right time because of the distributors only. There are different types of distribution methods, the advantages and disadvantages of each one of them are discussed below:

Own Shop

There are many producers like Bata etc which manages their own retail outlets. These retail stores ensure the right quality product at the right time to the right consumer. Since the company is selling products directly to the consumer so the feedback if any received from the end user is genuine. These shops along with selling the core products of the company also sell some complementary products to increase the range of the products.

Franchise Outlets

This type of network is fast catching up because the franchisee does not need to invest in the marketing activities. The franchiser gives legal rights to franchisee to run the entity as an independent business. The franchisees help the franchiser helps in giving better geographic coverage and increased market share.

Mail Order

Some of the products like magazines like Readers Digest, Mobile phone in special occasions etc are sold through Mail Order. The interested Customers are advised to send their request for the product directly to the manufacturer, who in turn provides the product directly to the end consumers.

Catalogue Sales

The catalogue sales are a variant of mail order; in this the firm attracts the consumer by providing them with attractive colorful products describing the features and quality of the product. These attractive and colorful catalogues are dispersed amongst large number of buyers, who then chooses the desired products from the catalogue and place the order for the product with the manufacturer. In the catalogue sales the firm has to ensure that the product quality as mentioned in the catalogue should conform as per the catalogue otherwise, the negative publicity about the product will dilute the firm's image.

Web Marketing

The advent of e-commerce has completely transformed the way the products are sold to the end consumer. The advancement in the technology and spread of computers and mobiles along with cheap data plans has opened new vistas for marketing and selling the product. The web marketing is the easiest way to order the products on the web with many services which were till now unheard of in the transaction process. The availability of easy finances and cash on delivery has made this online shopping very attractive amongst the young customers. The seller's ensure that the dispatch of the product is made with in the requisite time. They also offer deep discounts which increase the attractiveness of this type of shopping. The only disadvantage with this type of shopping is that the customer is not able to try the product physically and sometimes the product is not received as ordered which consumes lots of time in returning and again getting the desired product.

Agency Operation

The Agents operate independently and helps the manufacturers in selling their products to the final consumers. The agents directly receive orders from the customers, which are then forwarded to the manufacturers for making available the desired product to the consumer. When the transaction is complete the agent gets a commission which is called as agency commission. The agents work on the terms and conditions as decided with the manufacturer at the time of the contract. The main tasks of the agent are to negotiate the sales with the consumers on behalf of the company. They are able to build long-term mutual beneficial relationships with the consumers as the consumers get good products at reasonable prices on a consistent basis.

Stockists

The companies in many situations appoint stockists who provide the companies with the storage space. The job of the stockiest is to maintain stocks on behalf of the company and delivers the same to the distributor on getting instructions from the company. For providing the storage space and their efforts the stockiest get a commission from the producer. The stockiest are not directly involved in actual selling for the company.

Consignment Agents

The consignment agents are especially needed when a product is new to the market and the sale ability of the product is a question mark. They keep stocks of manufacturers' merchandise and they sell the products the money received is sent to the manufacturer. They are paid a commission on sales and their efforts. The selection of the channel depends on market survey, which guides the producer about the customer preferences and purchase patterns. Main criteria of the distribution channel are as follows:

1. Customer reaches for the channel.
2. Customer convenience of buying.
3. The availability of the service facility with the channel.
4. Products available from one manufacturer for the channel

Rural Market Segmentation

Rural market segmentation is the process of converting a heterogeneous market into a homogenous market. Market segmentation is dividing a market into small segments with similar needs and preferences. Rural market segmentation is the first step in the formulation of marketing strategies. After the market segmentation, the segment is chosen as per the competencies of the company and then is targeted with the marketing mix. The most common problem faced in segmenting the rural market is its heterogeneous nature. After targeting the product is positioned in the target market. Positioning is about creating a distinct image of the product in the minds of the customer. The segmentation of the market should be carried out very carefully as it can make or mar the marketing strategy of the companies. Market segmentation is the most potent tool in the hands of the marketer. There are different definitions of market segmentation given by experts but some of the most prominent among them are as follows:

The American Marketing Association defines market segmentation as a process of dividing the heterogeneous markets into smaller segments having homogeneous characteristics that can be satisfied by the firm."

Philip Kotler in his book marketing management defines market segmentation as the process of dividing the market into homogeneous subsets of consumers, and then this homogenous subset is targeted with a distinct marketing mix."

Rural Market Segmentation: Important Characteristics

It is very difficult for the marketer to satisfy all the segments in the market. Therefore, before selecting the market segment it is important to carefully evaluate the needs and preferences of the market segment. A market segment to be profitable should have the following characteristics they are:

1. Measurable

The market segment should not be too big and too small. It must have an appropriate size which can be measured in terms of data so that the market risk and potential can be calculated. The market segment should be distinct, clear and measurable. If the market segment is not measurable then it becomes a futile exercise. Now a day the rural markets are being studied by most of the marketing companies to get the relevant data which would help in effective market segmentation.

2. Accessible

The market segment should be accessible at a cost that is affordable to the company. Accessibility is the reach of the company to the market segment. The market segment must be conveniently reachable to the company to satisfy the needs of the customer. Marketers prefer the segment of the urban market because of the better infrastructure in the urban areas as compared to the rural market segments. But lately due to better infrastructure and connectivity in rural areas also the rural markets are becoming increasingly accessible. The market Segments must be accessible due to two main reasons, firstly, the customers should be aware of products and services and secondly, the customer should get the products as at the right place, right time and at the right price.

3. Differentiable

The different market segments chosen by the company should have distinct characteristics so that they are differentiable. Each segment should have distinguishing features. The Rural market segments responses differ from urban market segments for many products.

For Example – In the case of a bike the rural consumers give more importance to strength and average of the bike, whereas urban consumers look for features and aesthetics.

4. Substantial

The market segment should be substantial in size so that it remains profitable. The market segment should either consist of large numbers of consumers who are light users or the market segment should have a small number of consumers with heavy usage so that the segment is profitable to the company. Since the Rural areas are heterogeneous it becomes difficult for the companies to design different marketing strategies.

5. Actionable or Feasible

Each market segment chosen by the companies must be actionable which means that the company should have sufficient finance, marketing personnel's and capability to serve the market segment. Therefore, the market segments should be selected, base on the reach of the company.

6. Other Considerations

Apart from the above characteristics, the market segment of the company must be profitable and should have the least risks and competition. The segment should be stable suitable, practicable and attractive to the firm. The company should have the resources to satisfy the market segment effectively. The various instructions and guidelines issued by the government from time to time should also be given due importance.

Bases of Rural Market Segmentation

The market can be segmented on four main bases they are geographic, demographic, behavioral and psychographic characteristics. Each one of the bases is explained in detail.

1. Geographic Location

Geographic Location is segmenting the market based on geography; this is one of the popular bases for market segmentation. Broadly the market can be segmented into Urban and rural market segments. The urban markets are more concentrated as compared to the rural markets. Companies like Hindustan Unilever Limited have been able to target the rural segment by building a strong retail network in the villages. Apart from this, the market can be segmented on the bases of regions like South, West, East and North, country, state, city or even neighborhood. Different climatic conditions define the buying patterns in different geographic segments.

2. Demographic Segmentation

The main attributes used for demographic segmentation are Age, ethnicity, Life stage, Gender, income Religion, and nationality. Demographic segmentation helps in categorization the need of the customer. In the present scenario, the children have high awareness about new products and act as a strong influence in the buying decisions of the family. Therefore, the marketers are targeting the youths for different kind of products. This type of segmentation helps the companies in spending their marketing budget more efficiently. Various analytics software's are used for demographic segmentation.

3. Behavioural Segmentation

Behavioural segmentation is segmenting the total market based on consumer buying behaviour. Behavioural segmentation is concerned with buying patterns like usage frequency, brand loyalty benefits needed; occasion etc. This type of segmentation is done keeping in mind the needs and wants of the consumer based on their buying behaviour patterns.

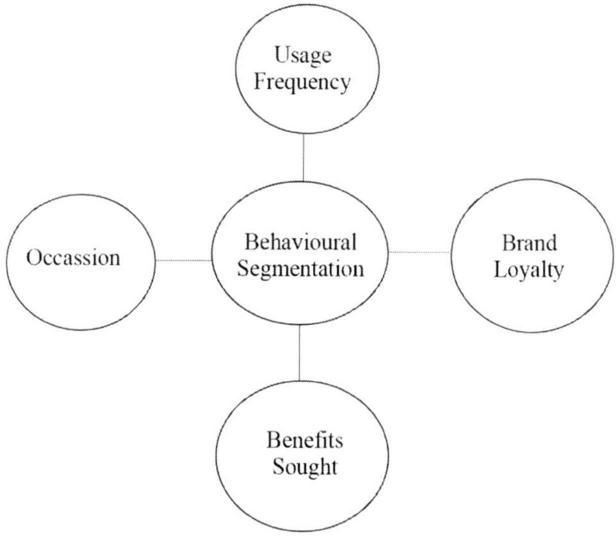

Fig. 3.3: Behavioural Segmentation Variables (Kotler, 2012)

4. Psychographic Segmentation

Psychographic segmentation which was developed in 1971 is used to segment the market based on shared psychological characteristics, consumer attitudes, motivations, to and explain predict consumer behaviour. Psychographic segmentation is a method which uses variables like personality traits, beliefs, values, attitudes, and lifestyles for segmenting the market. These characteristics may be abstract or observable. This type of segmentation is very different from other segmentation methods. But it complements demographic and socioeconomic segmentation and enables the marketers to build their marketing communications accordingly. Every customer/consumer has a unique psychographic makeup. For the urban and rural segments, it is very different. When the target segment has different needs and responses to the offering then it indicates that the process of psychographic segmentation has to start. This segmentation is an important method to offer the same product to customers who seems heterogeneous. The psychographic segmentation yields the greatest payoff, in terms of purchase frequency, lifetime loyalty, and more. The other method which is used by marketers to segment the market is based on the degree of which are as follows:

1. Mass Marketing

Mass marketing is based on a philosophy in which one product is offered to the whole market using the same marketing mix. Initially, mass marketing was used for the rural markets in which it was believed the needs of the rural consumer are the same. But as the rural market started evolving and the consumer became more demanding mass marketing can have its limitations. In this case, the company does not feel the need for segmentation. Mass marketing is also known as an undifferentiated marketing strategy. For example: Bisleri water bottles.

2. Segment Marketing

Segment marketing is still in its early stages in rural markets. The companies have realized the importance of segmenting the market. Companies like Hindustan Unilever limited use of different approaches to market their brands for example–Hamam and Lifebuoy. The Company tries to reach the whole market by using the mass marketing approach for its brand Hamam whereas four variants of its Lifebuoy – Active Red, Active Orange, Plus and Gold – are marketed to the different segments of the Indian market.

3. Niche Marketing

A Niche is a very small segment with a distinct and complex set of needs. In the fashion industry, there might be segments like regular wear, party and for fashion shows; different types of clothes which constitutes a niche are required. In the niches, the competition is very less there are few or no competitors and the product commands a premium price. Unlike mass audiences, which represent a large number of people, a niche audience is an influential smaller audience. For example: Designer Clothes.

4. Micro Marketing

Micromarketing refers to the customization of products for the tightly targeted group. Micromarketing occurs when the needs of the small segment are addressed on a local basis. The examples of micro marketing are Dabur's Anmol Hair Oil, mustard amla bases oil launched for northern Indian markets of a small pack, targeted at rural consumers using loose mustard oil. Micro Marketing includes local marketing and individual marketing.

(a) Local Marketing

Local marketing involves designing products to meet the requirements of the local customer on a geographical basis. Local marketing is most relevant for rural consumers. It is a marketing strategy that targets customers on the basis location such as a city or neighborhood. It is used by local businesses to reach the customers nearest to them. A local company uses specific marketing strategies to target customers related to its segment. Local brands are very good at local marketing since they operate in a limited geography, which helps them to develop a good understanding of local consumers and their specific needs.

(b) Individual Marketing

Individual marketing is also called as one to one marketing. The rural marketers are shifting from local marketing to Individual marketing for example, with the use of computer-aided design and computer- aided manufacturing; it has now become possible to manufacture a product as per the individual customer needs. Tailoring is the examples of individual marketing in the rural set-up. In individual marketing, an individual can get a product according to his/her specific needs.

5. Target Marketing

A target market is a subset of the total market for a product or service. Target Marketing is breaking the market into small segments and then concentrating all the marketing strategies on these segments, depending on how closely the need matches with the offerings. Target marketing is a modern marketing concept. Target marketing helps the company to effectively identify the target market for which the product is designed. Two approaches can be followed for target marketing. First is o treat the target market as a single unit using a single marketing mix and secondly, when the market has different segments and the consumer is targeted using different marketing mixes. Thus, in target marketing, the companies can choose the strategy of no market segmentation or complete market segmentation depending upon the companies approach.

5.1 Rural Communication and Distribution systems

Rural Communication has gained great importance in the changing marketing scenarios more specifically in rural areas. Effective communication plays an important role in transmitting the right message to the target segment. It also increases the reach of the product in rural areas. It is therefore important to understand the key concepts of communications in rural areas.

The Communication Process Model

The process of communication starts with a clear message which is encoded, a sender sends this encoded message using a transmission medium, to the receiver which the receiver receives and decodes the message. The receiver sends the feedback to the sender which helps in the improvement of the message. In the communication model the noise act as a barrier in the flow of communication which should be minimized. Noise can happen due to message not decoded properly or the wrong selection of media. Noise can lead to distortion of information therefore it should be avoided.

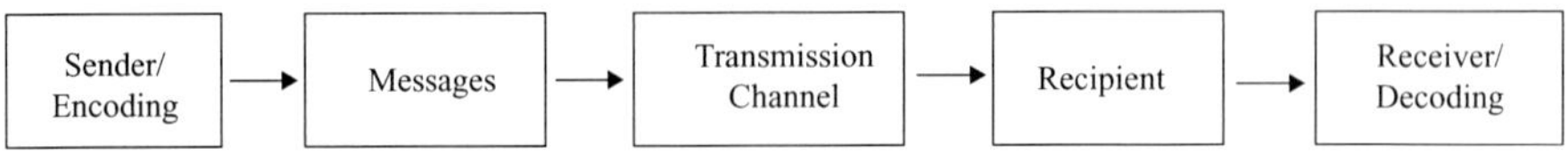

Fig. 3.4 Elements of communication process. *Source*: Gronroos, (2004)

The main challenge for the companies operating in the rural market is how to make the message understandable and interesting to them. There are several factors which make a message effective and interesting. The message created for the rural customer should be meaningful to the rural consumer. The various factors which make the message effective are as follows:

Languages: The message should be created in the language which is understood by the receiver. This means that the language used in the message should be simple and unambiguous words are used.

Pictorial Presentation: Since the literacy level of rural customers is low the pictures and graphics must be used extensively in the message. It makes the message interesting and easy to understand. The pictorial presentation includes the use of cartoons, colours, symbols and logos.

Message form: In an effective communication process the message should be utilitarian i.e. having some utility and narrative.

Source of the Message: The Credibility of the source for effective communication is very important for the rural consumer. The source which is not credible would not have an impact on the consumer.

Context Association: The context Associations should create interest, hold the attention of the consumer and provide relevant meaning. Some of the influencers in the context association are products of interest to the rural consumer, aesthetics and settings.

Types of Media

For communicating with the consumer the media plays an important role. The effectiveness of communication depends on the selection of the media channel. Broadly media can be classified into two types:

- Mass Media or conventional media and
- Non-conventional media.

Mass or Conventional Media

Mass media includes those mediums which have mass appeals like television with satellite channels, radio, print media, cinema, word of mouth and video vans which play videos with product informatio. etc. The mass media plays an important role in the rural markets but the effectiveness of the non-conventional media which includes Puppetry shows, Folk theatres, demonstrations, Haats, wall paintings and Fairs etc, cannot be downplayed for the rural audience. Various factors which are important for media effectiveness are:

- Target segment profile
- Media preferences
- Programmes viewed; and
- Consumer Behaviour

Non-Conventional Media

Non conventional media: The non electronic mediums which work as a part of culture and work as a vehicle for transmitting tradition from one generation to another is called non conventional or traditional media. Some of the examples of the non conventional media are listed as below:

- Wall paintings
- Direct mail
- Banners placed on elephants parading through main bazaars
- Puppetry
- Processions, tableaus, float, etc.
- Contexts to promote the products
- Audiovisual vans
- Stalls, hoardings and audio-visual publicity at local fairs
- Point-of-purchase channels
- Demonstration and sampling at haats and fairs.

Communication with rural consumers can be done effectively with non-conventional media. Puppetry shows, drama, messages on objects of interest, and giant cut-outs generates interest in the rural consumers. Interactive communication at contact points at 'Haats' and 'Melas' creates brand knowledge and awareness and influences the buying behaviour of the consumers.

Rural Communication-Challenges and Strategies

The marketers are faced with several challenges in rural communication. The following section presents some of these challenges, and strategies faced by the marketer.

- **Spread and Diversity:** A large number of rural consumers are scattered across the country and they have no access to the mass media or traditional media.
- Low Literacy Levels of rural consumers:
- **Poor Infrastructure Facilities:** Such as lack of roads, electricity, telecom facilities, postal services, etc.
- **Unique Media Habits:** Almost all the readership is secondary, the press subscription is low and magazines are not read in rural areas.
- **Low-Spending Capacity:** Rural consumers have low disposable incomes to buy products.
- **Lack of Research Data:** Most of the marketing decisions are largely dependent on feedback from sales networks.
- **Selective Attention:** Messages are given selective attention by rural population this problem is compounded by low product-availability.
- **Linguistic and Socio-cultural differences:** Language and socio-cultural, norms differ from village to village creating problems for the marketer in designing the message.
- **Orthodox Societies:** In most of the rural areas the societies are male-dominated and they are influencer and buyers of products. So the role of women is very limited.
- **Different Leisure Time Activities:** The rural population is predominantly engaged in agricultural activities to have no fixed timings. Therefore, the time slot for the ads becomes a challenge for the marketer for achieving mass population.

Rural Distribution

According to the census of 2011 Rural India consists of 627,000 villages, 629 million people. This is a huge market which offers immense opportunities to marketers. Many big companies such as Hindustan Lever, Colgate-Palmolive and Philips have been trying to entice the rural consumers. The opportunity is huge as 12 per cent of the world's population, or 126 million households, lives in rural India. With the better-earning opportunities, rural consumers have the purchasing power. Between 30 and 50 per cent of the consumption of consumer goods comes from rural India. The marketing communications were not given much importance as compared with the urban markets, but now the big companies are investing huge sums of money in the rural communications also, but there are challenges to marketing communication in the rural markets. These challenges have a direct bearing on the distribution activities. Due to the high distribution costs, the companies have started innovations to make distribution more effective. Most of the distribution problems are due to poor transport and communication facilities, scattered village settlements, and small retail outlets having modest sales. With the changing scenario, there are many retail outlets in the country which are located in the rural areas. They offer a range of products, from biscuits to pharmaceuticals, to shop shelves in different parts of the country. Now the companies are taking distribution into their own hands, by developing their own dedicated, focused channels.

The Village Retailers

The rural retail system is an important mechanism to satisfy the requirements of the rural consumer. The rural retail system has the maximum reach to rural consumers. The main functions of the village retailers are:

- To ensure that the right product reaches the rural retail outlet at the right time
- To persuade the rural retailer to inventories a product. It is important as more dealers' results in maximum reach among consumer and, therefore, a higher market share.

This can be achieved by understanding the influences on rural distribution systems. Some of the influencing factors are:

- Purchase behaviour of consumers;
- Characteristics of retailers; and
- Channel Behaviour.

Purchase Behaviour of Consumer

The consumer purchase behaviour is influenced by the rural retailer who is instrumental in creating brand knowledge in rural consumers, and enjoys the trust of rural consumer. 'Mannerisms' of the retailer plays an important role in developing long term relationships with the customers. Companies like Gillette are already focusing on this aspect of mannerisms to tap the rural market.

Characteristics of Retailers

- Rural markets are scattered which increases the distribution costs of the retailer and this acts as a deterrent for entry of new products in rural markets.
- Retail premises are mostly rented.
- Retail shelf, many a time's offers sub-standard or me too types of products as compared to the urban areas.
- Stock turnover is low-posing a challenge for the Retailer.

Channel Behaviour (Retailer)

- **Credit facilities to the customer** by the rural retailer are common in rural settings.
- **Pricing:** Some retailers often overcharge, not posing on discounts to customers.
- **Reasons for stocking the product:** Either demand or wholesaler's push.
- **Information and influence sources:** The wholesalers and retailers both share information and influence each other.
- **Purchase source:** The rural retailers travel down to feeder towns for supplies.
- **Channel credit:** Village retailers avail credit facilities offered by distributors in feeder markets.
- **Channel promotion:** Retailers in feeder markets avail more discounts as compared to retailers in interior villages, for they prefer not to stock more.
- **Promotion by the retailer**: Due to strong bonding with the customer's retailers have a great influence on the buyer; the retailers are also influenced by the commission on the sales.

Haats and Fairs

'Haats' and fairs, held regularly, provide an opportunity for marketers to access rural consumers. Since they are weekly events a large number of rural consumers come here to purchase the products.

'Haats': 'Haats' are weekly periodic markets, organized is an open-air market that serves as a trading venue for rural people in the interior of rural markets. Haat bazaars are organized to support or promote trading by and with rural people. The haats reaches the remotest rural consumer in large numbers. There are 47,000 'haats' (Kashyap, 1998) held periodically in rural India. Rural consumers congregate weekly at a particular 'place', to buy or sell products. This setting is known as a 'haat'. Large haats are held at large 'places' whereas smaller ones at small places. The 'haats' are organized on a rented location at a nominal price. India's Largest Haat Bazaar is Gohpur Haat Bazaar from Gohpur in Assam.

There are different types of traders in these 'haats' which are as follows:

- **Part-Time Traders**
- **Producer-Sellers**
- **Collector-Sellers:** They collect leaves, firewood, grass for fodder, etc., for sales.
- **Full-time Trader:** Full-time traders in these 'Haats' comprise of three classes: the selling traders, the buying-traders, and service-providers.
- **Selling-Traders:** Selling-Traders are those that sell goods.
- **Buying-Traders:** They buy from the haat to sell somewhere else or at some other time.
- **Service-Providers:** They are engaged in services, including barbers, blacksmiths, carpenters, tea stall owners etc.

Melas (Fairs)

Mela is a Sanskrit word meaning 'gathering' or 'to meet' .It is used in India for all types of gatherings which can be religious, commercial, or cultural."Mela" is popularly known as fairs, shows and exhibitions. The melas can be an important platform for promoting culture, art or skill. About 70% of the visitors in the Melas come from nearby villages. These melas provide a golden opportunity to the marketers to showcase their brands to the rural consumers. Generally, in "melas" people can find eateries, entertainment activities and shops. Melas offer opportunity for long term marketing tie-ups with wholesalers and traders. These fairs are organized at specific places, on festivals to commemorate important festivals. Rural people participate in these fairs, and sell their excess produce. Villagers along with their families spend wholeheartedly in these fairs. These fairs offer a good opportunity for marketers to launch new products and promote existing products. Some of the biggest 'melas' are Kumbh, Pushkar, trade fairs etc. The difference between Haats and melas is that Haats caters to primary needs of the local people whereas melas cater to the larger population both urban and rural. Haats and melas are important mediums for the marketer to sell and promote its product.

Direct Distribution: Alternative Rural Distribution Strategy

Now a day's most of the marketers are trying to reduce the number of intermediaries in the supply chain. The reason for this is that it cuts the costs of the company and most of the times the true picture of the market is not portrayed by the intermediary. To overcome this problem most of the companies have now started to directly approach the customers with their product. The marketers now believe that direct distribution can give them the exact picture of the market and guarantee them rural success. The companies have limited control over the wholesalers although the wholesale channel costs less than direct distribution in rural markets. The Wholesalers prefer big brands in which they have higher margins, they avoid the new products because the margins are less and the market share of the product is low. The wholesalers do not support new products. Due to these reasons, the companies prefer direct distribution although the cost in the direct distribution is higher it allows better control over the quality of the distribution. Due to the above point, it can be concluded that the companies go for direct distribution in the rural markets because of three main reasons:

- Direct distribution in rural markets becomes critical when the market is competitive and the products or services offered by the competitor are comparable with the existing players.
- Direct distribution also becomes critical if there are a large number of new products especially for the rural markets; and
- Direct distribution is least important for the markets in which there is no competition and there is no possibility of immediate competitor threat.

Role of Agricultural Produce Marketing Committees

Agricultural Produce Market Committee (APMC) is a statutory market committee constituted by a State Government for trading notified agricultural, horticultural or livestock products, under the APMC Act of the state government. The Agricultural produce marketing committees are responsible for:

- Ensuring transparency in the pricing system and transactions;
- Providing market-led extension services to farmers;
- Ensuring payment on the same day for agricultural produce;
- Promoting and processing activities for value addition in agricultural produce;
- Publicizing data on arrivals and rates of agricultural produce;
- Promoting public-private partnership in the management of agricultural markets.

There are approximately 2477 regulated markets and 4843 sub-market regulated by the respective APMCs in India. The APMC's provides basic amenities in and around the APMCs like auction halls,

weighbridges, godowns, shops, canteens, lights, drinking water, toilets, police station, post-office, bore- wells, warehouse, tanks, Water Treatment plant, soil-testing Laboratory, toilet blocks, etc.

Functions of APMC

As already discussed in the responsibility of APMC's there are various functions which are undertaken by the APMC's. The main functions are:

1. To promote public-private partnership in the ambit of agricultural markets.
2. To provide market-led extension services to the farmer.
3. To keep an eye on the pricing system and transactions taking place in the market in a transparent manner.
4. To ensure payments to the farmers for the sale of agricultural produce on the same day.
5. To promote agricultural activities.

To announce data on arrivals and rates of agricultural produce from time to time into the market.

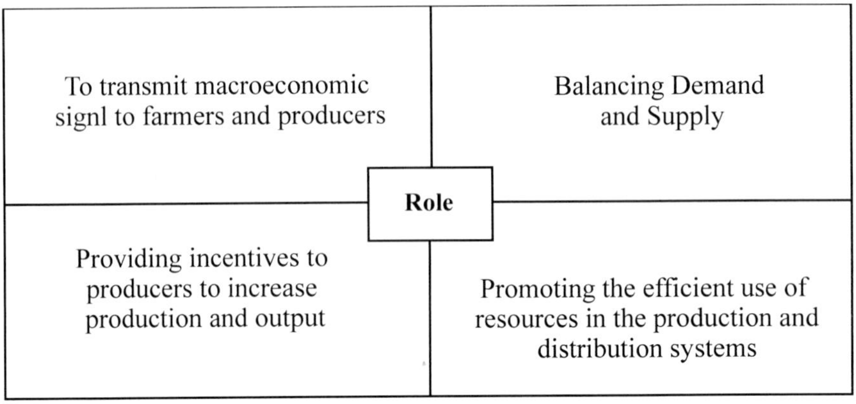

Fig. 3.5: Role of Agricultural Produce Marketing Committee *Source*: Kadrolkar, (2011)

Functioning of APMCs: Issues Involved

The APMC act was introduced in 2003 to prevent the farmers against exploitation by the intermediaries and creditors have successfully minimized the farmer's distress but there are some issues which need to be taken in to account for making the act more effective. The APMC act ensures better and timely payment for their produce through the auctions in the APMC area. APMC act restricts the farmer from entering into a direct contract with any processor or manufacturer as the agricultural produce is to be sold through these regulated markets only. The major issues involved in the functioning of APMCs is that over some time the APMC controlled markets have acquired the status of restrictive and Monopolistic markets, harming the farmers rather than helping them to get better prices for their produce. The APMC Act levies the market fee as the tax levied by the state, rather than as a fee charged for providing services, which is a major issue in creating a national common market. APMCs charge a market fee from buyers, and a licensing fee from the commissioning agents who mediate between buyers and farmers. They also charge small licensing fees from agents, loading agents etc. These levies vary from state to state. Apart from these fees statutory levies/mandi tax,etc. all add up to hefty amounts, which creates market distortions and have cascading effects on the profits of the farmers and act as strong entry barriers for many stakeholders. The multiple licenses and fees have led to a highly fragmented and high- cost agricultural economy, which prevents economies of scale and free movement of agricultural products across district and state borders. The opaque system of fee collection, which are at times is exorbitant, is not under the state legislature's approval. Agents in an APMC may get together and form a cartel which creates a monopsony situation (one buyer who then exercises control over the price at which he buys). The agricultural produce is procured at the manipulative price and sold at a higher price, defeating the very purpose of APMCs. APMCs play the twin role of regulator and Market. Therefore, the role of APMC as a regulator is undermined by vested interest. The key positions of chairman and members of APMCs are nominated/elected out of the agents operating in that market. As the exporters and retail chain operators cannot directly procure the agricultural products from the farmers as the products need to be regulated through regulated markets, in this process, there is a huge increase in the marketing costs and the farmers end up getting a low price for their produce. Policies of the state- controlled markets have prevented private investment in the sector. Thus, this monopoly has made the market non-competitive on a pan-India basis, which hinders the process of organized retail and smooth raw material supply to agro-processing industries. The monopolistic practices have acted as a strong barrier in the adoption of innovative marketing system and technologies.

5

Communication Technology in Rural Marketing

Introduction

The communication which is the core of the Communication Mix plays an important role in promoting the product to the outside world and especially to the target market. In the marketing of rural products, application of latest, innovative and enhanced technologies is crucial for effective communication with urban consumers. This also helps in conveying the features of rural products. The adoption of the latest technologies ensures the economic well-being of the rural marketers by increasing the reach of the products and in creating awareness about the product. The technology helps in faster dissemination of the rural product information to the consumer. Effective usage of information and communication technologies can do wonders for the rural marketers. The government under its flagship program of digital India is focusing on developing the technology infrastructure in the rural areas. The development of the ICT infrastructure would lead to better advertising of the rural products which in turn helps in the economic growth of the rural marketers. The economic growth of the company and the advertising efforts works in close coordination with each other. Due to economic liberalization prosperity of the Indian buyers have increased manifold and the marketers are increasingly trying to outdo other marketers through their promotion activities

Market Communication and Channels

Marketing communication is the process which includes informing, influencing consumers to make a purchase decision about a particular product. The marketing communication which is an important element of the Communication Mix focuses on three main points: firstly, to inform the consumers; secondly, to persuade the consumer; and thirdly, to convince the consumer to take the desired action. Effective marketing communication equips companies with a competitive edge to survive in the competitive environment. Marketing communication is a type of non-price competition where the competition is not in terms of price but the product features. marketing communications serve three main functions, they are:

1. Informative communication
2. Persuasive communication
3. Reminding the consumer forms of marketing communication have been briefly described below:

Advertising

Advertising is a means of mass communication. The American Marketing Association defines Advertising as any paid form of promotion of ideas or goods by an identified sponsor. Advertising is a paid form of non-personal communication for the promotion of goods, ideas and services by an identified sponsor. The advertisements can be made in house or with the help of an external advertising agency. Advertising is used to:

- Reach large Audiences
- Create brand awareness
- Helps in differentiating brands form competitors.

Publicity

Publicity is also a non-personal communication for the stimulation of demand stimulation for a particular product or service generally in some media form. Mass media like the radio, television etc are important means of publicity. The publicity is not paid for by the company. The publicity can be negative or positive which can create positive or negative perceptions for a brand.

Some of the key points of publicity are as follows:

- Non paid form of communication
- Provides information about a company or product.

Personal Selling

According to Philip Kotler personal selling is face to face interaction with one or more prospective purchasers for the purposes of making the sales. Personal selling is the oldest forms of communication with the prospect of increasing the sales of the product. In personal selling, the company representative can interact with more prospects at the same time and can answer their queries then and there. The problem with personal selling is this that it is very time consuming, have limited reach, and expensive method.

Sales Promotion

According to American Marketing Association sales promotion is defined as media and non-media marketing pressure applied for a predetermined, limited period of time in order to stimulate trial and impulse purchases, increase consumer demand or improve products quality. Sales promotion includes those activities which are not covered by advertising, publicity and personal selling to increase the sales of the particular brand. Sales promotion activities include public displays, celebrity endorsement, shows and expositions, exhibitions, demonstrations in colleges or universities and many other innovative selling efforts at the purchase points and other non-recurrent selling efforts not in the ordinary routine. Sales promotion complements other forms of marketing communications. All the marketing communications plays the role of an important link of communication between the marketers and the prospect. As already discussed the main objectives of promotion are:

a. Information

b. Persuasion

c. Reminding

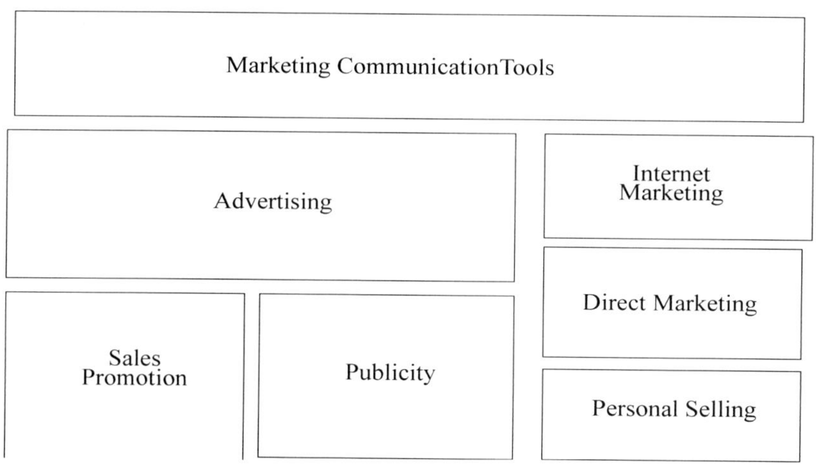

Marketing Communication Tools
Source: Schultz, D. E., & Schultz, H. F. (1998)

The marketing communication is a wider concept in marketing which also includes:

- The conveying of product personality which encompasses the brand name, brand equity, packaging and labelling.

- To convey the Pricing importance conveying quality, status, unique features.
- Encompasses the promotion-mix which covers personal selling, advertising, publicity, and sales promotion.
- Place or distribution which indicates the point of purchase, store image, merchandise presentation and services.

Thus, all the elements of the Communication Mix communicate with the consumer with the marketing messages. Of the four elements of the Communication, Mix promotion is the most visible element of marketing communication. Without this element, it is impossible to compete in the marketing environment.

The customer-initiated marketing communication model propounds that the companies should use create such information channels which helps in creating long term relationship with the consumers and which provides reliable and genuine feedback so that the feedback leads to the improvement in the product. Now a day with the rapid penetration of the internet every individual is interconnected. The customer-initiated marketing communication model given by Duncan (2005) starts with a source providing information through several channels to the company through the noise. Feedback is an important component of this model. The model explains the one-on-one communication method between the consumer and the company and also suggest for private communication with the consumer.

Diagrammatically this model can be represented as shown below:

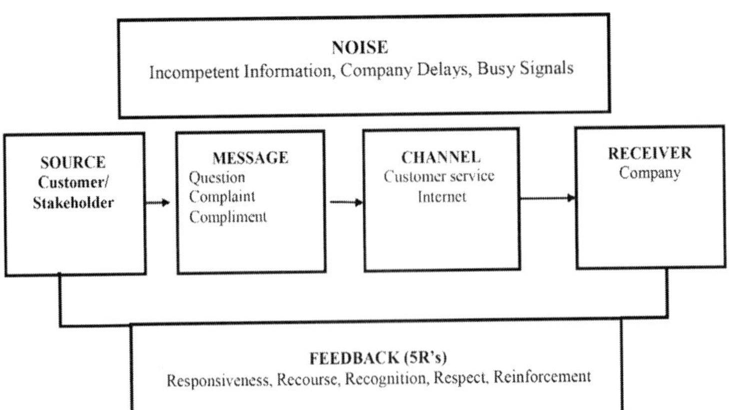

Customer-Initiated Marketing Communication Model
Source: Duncan (2005)

As the model suggests the marketing communication has three main requirements which are listed below:

- To identify the best possible medium to ensure the maximum geographical reach.
- Customer profiling and understanding the characteristics of the target markets.
- To formulate the best promotional strategy so that the buying behaviour of the consumers is effectively influenced.

To conclude the objectives of the Marketing communications for a company are long-term which focuses on increasing the brand value and brand equity of a brand over time.

Determining Marketing Communication Objectives

To use marketing communication in promotional activities, the marketers go through several steps to achieve the communication objectives. The steps involved in the development of an effective marketing communication campaign are:

4. Identification of the target market
5. Determining the objectives of the Marketing Campaign
6. The setting of S.M.A.R.T. goals
7. Define and create the message
8. Selection of marketing communications tools.
9. Determining the promotional mix
10. Execute the marketing campaign
11. Measure results and Feedback.

Determine Target Market

The target market is the market which the companies focus on with their marketing activities, because of its competency. A clearly defined target market helps the companies in designi communications for effectively reaching their target market.

Determine Marketing Campaign Objectives

This step identifies the objectives of the company which it wants to achieve through its marketing campaign. The marketing communications of the company tries to accomplish more objectives at a time. The marketing campaign of the company focuses on creating brand awareness amongst the target market and influences their buying behaviour. In developing marketing campaigns the AIDA model is a useful tool for the achievement of campaign objectives for the target market.

The AIDA Model

AIDA is an acronym of attention, interest, desire and action. It helps marketers to develop effective marketing communication strategies to connect with the target market. AIDA model was given by EliasSt. Elmo Lewis. marketing communication. The acronym AIDA acronym stands for:

- **A** represents attention or awareness, and the ability to attract the attention of the consumers.
- **I** raise the interest of consumers by focusing on advantages and benefits.
- **D** represents desire and convinces consumers that the product will satisfy their needs.
- **A** is an action leading to actual purchase.

AIDA Model
(*Source*: Essential marketing models http://bit.ly/Smartmodels)

Set S.M.A.R.T Goals

In the marketing campaigns, the marketers should set specific goals using S.M.A.R.T. criteria which are in sync with the marketing strategy. Acronym S.M.A.R.T. was given by George T. Doran. George T. Doran proposed that goals should be:

- Specific
- Measurable
- Assignable
- Realistic
- Timely

S.M.A.R.T goals will help ensure clarity in the activities that needs to carry out for marketing campaign. They also contribute to good communication between managers and employees, so that there are clear expectations on all sides about the focus of attention, resources, and results.

Define and Create the Message

Defining and creating the message guides the marketer in developing a message framework to get the message right. The main objective of the message is the call to action. The calls to action should follow the AIDA model and influence the audience by using the tools effectively.

Selecting the Marketing Communication Methods

The marketing communications are formulated with a purpose to have maximum impact on the consumers. For this purpose, some important factors are kept in consideration which shapes the choices of the marketers in the formulation of marketing communications. These factors are as follows:

Budget: The budget for the marketing campaign and what resources are available to the marketer determines the effectiveness of the marketing campaign. A big-budget can incorporate the usage of latest technologies whereas limited budget makes the marketer compromise on many things. The marketer needs to analyze the impact of the available budget.

Timing: Some Integrated Marketing Communication methods and tactics such as conference presentations and events require a significantly longer lead time than others to orchestrate whereas email and web marketing activities can be executed rapidly with in-house resources. It is very important to choose the right tools that will make the biggest impact in the available time.

Audience: Effective marketing communications reach the consumer where they are. The media habits and behaviours of the target segments guide marketer's choice for the budget, tools which are used around marketing communication.

Assessing the Organizational Strengths: When developing the marketing communications, the marketers should look for its internal strengths and weaknesses and should make the best use of its strengths to effectively connect with the consumer. The strengths of the marketing companies provide the competitive advantages that competitors cannot easily match or replicate. The table below illustrates different tools of marketing communication which are being used by marketers.

Tools of Marketing Communications

S. No.	Marketing Communications Tools
1	Advertising
2	Public Relations
3	Promotions
4	Word of Mouth
5	Corporate Communications
6	Sponsorship
7	Exhibitions and Fairs

Road Shows

A road show is a promotional activity which includes series of presentations carried out at different locations for offering a product or service. The road show is a process of sales pitch which involves members of the company which travel around the country offering the opportunity. The main purpose of road show is to generate excitement and interest in the offering. A successful road show is critical to the success of the offering. Road show events attract hundreds of prospective buyers interested in learning more about the offering. The Road show events include multimedia presentations and question-and-answer sessions with company's executives. Many companies use technology to post videos of the road shows and online presentations. Along with Road shows companies may also hold smaller, private meetings with the prospects. Road shows cover a variety of areas like the company's history and their future plans. The road shows include the following:

- A video or digital media presentation
- Company's history and how it got started
- Meeting the executive management
- Plans and vision for the company
- The unique value proposition of the company
- Earnings and financial performance
- Prior sales growth with projections and forecasts
- The investment opportunity and growth potential
- IPO stock price target

Challenges in Marketing Communication

Every organization operating in the market faces challenges which it needs to overcome. Similarly, the companies face many challenges in implementing the effective marketing campaign also. The major challenges which the company faces are finding the right kind of talented human resources and the right technology. But there is scope for overcoming these challenges by redesigning the strategies related to marketing communications. The companies should be ready to face these challenges head-on. The dissemination of information through different marketing channels increases the burden on marketing professional to effectively optimize the marketing channels. Use of offline and online communication does not guarantee symmetry in communication. It can be challenged if the marketing communication is not directed at the right customer. Therefore the marketers must determine which channels should be focused on to distinguish between noise and message. The companies which are operating in foreign countries face considerable communication challenges. It must be kept in mind that marketing communications reflects the local market requirements and take care of the cultural aspects before designing a message. The media used must deliver the message which is acceptable to local cultural preferences. Some of the important points which need to be taken into consideration to overcome the challenges in marketing communications are:

Localizing Communications

The marketer while promoting their product must communicate in the local language. This means the translation of the message into local languages. Apart from this the marketing communication should persuade the consumers that the needs and wants of the local buyers are met. The marketing communications must comply with the legal requirements of the host company.

Consistent Usage of Product Terminology

Another challenge for the marketer is that the marketer must ensure that the names of products are used consistently in every geographical location. Inconsistent usage of product names can create logistics problems in supplying the right product. Terminology management provides a solution to this problem by ensuring consistent communication.

Meeting Local Cultural Preferences

Local cultural preferences should be kept in inactive consideration. Using particular colours combinations and images creates a distinct image in the mind of the consumer.

Communicating Through the Right Channels

Apart from knowing how to communicate, marketers must know how and where to reach the end consumer. In some cases, participating in exhibitions and fairs may be the most effective route to reach to the final consumers. In such cases, orators with excellent communication and presentation skills should be used. Whereas in developed countries have established businesses, advertisements, news releases may be the most relevant form of communication. In cases where technology is not developed personal communication through distributors can be the best strategy. So, the main challenges in marketing communication can be summarized as follows:

- Generating Leads
- Providing ROI on Marketing Activities
- Securing adequate Budget
- Identifying the Right technologies of communication for the target market
- Managing the Website
- Targeting International Audience
- Training of the Team
- Hiring Top Talent

The companies have many options now to communicate with the target market. With the evolving information technologies, the way to communicate with the rural consumers has undergone a complete transformation. Engaging with the audience helps in generating new ideas, and gives ideas to the marketer for developing new products, or to modify and improve the existing products. Companies should take advantage of these innovations to interact with the consumer. marketing communications is to be flexible and make efficient use of the marketing communication tools, coordinating with the company's overall strategic objectives.

Role of Social Marketing in Marketing of Rural Goods

Social marketing is an important element of the Marketing process. It is one element which gained prominence in the last couple of decades. Social marketing was not given much importance by the companies till recently by most of the companies but now every company is trying to reach as many consumers as possible through social marketing for promotion of rural goods.

This concept of social marketing has gained momentum in the western countries in the 1970s due to the increased awareness about the concept of sustainability

Concept of Social Marketing

American marketing association defines marketing as the process of planning and executing the conception, pricing, promotion and distribution that satisfies individual and organizational goals. It is also a societal process by which individuals and groups obtain what they want through creating, offering and freely exchanging products and services of value with others. Social Marketing is defined as a process involves a change in the behaviour and attitudes of the target group for achieving the social, economic, political and business objectives. Social Marketing refers to creating awareness among consumers, organizations and the general public for the fulfillment of long term objectives of the company. Philip Kotler & Zaltman defined social marketing as the process of calculating the influence of efforts on the adoption of social ideas.

Social Marketing is also referred to as societal Marketing. Societal marketing is often referred to as a type of marketing in which the companies' profits are concentrated in such a way that it have minimum negative impact on the societies well being. Societal marketing also keeps in to account the well being of the plane earth. The main focus of social marketing is to achieve the following objectives:

- The satisfaction of customer needs.
- Improvement in the quality of life of the consumers
- Implementation of long term policy for customers and society's welfare
- To provide an environment-friendly system for the fulfillment of the consumer needs.

Aspects of Social Marketing

Looking at the harmful effects and environmental problems that marketing have caused is been noticed by the organizations. The harmful effects of irresponsible marketing have caused so much damage to the environment that it is becoming difficult to maintain the ecological balance. To offset these problems the companies have started adopting social marketing. Since societal marketing focuses on the societal aspects a social well being of the society, the important features of societal marketing can be summarized as follows, so that sociologists, the social leaders, the philanthropists and Marketers advocated social marketing. Over the past few years, marketing experts, practitioners have tried to identify basic aspects of (component) of social marketing. These can be summarized as under

Need-Based and Eco-Friendly Product Mix

The social marketing is about producing and marketing products in such a way that it causes a minimum harmful impact on the environment. Social marketing is about marketing essentially eco-friendly products. It should also communicate with consumers to convey the advantages of using eco-friendly products.

Rational Promotional Policy

Social marketing sells ideas, to promote, social products. In social marketing, the marketer uses advertising, public relations, door to door selling, etc. for emphasizing on the adoption of eco-friendly products. The social marketing ensures that the promotion of products is not antisocial and unethical. Social marketing is an effort to drive behaviour around a social issue.

Common Challenges in Rural Communication

The most successful social marketing efforts are those which understand customer's attitudes and beliefs. It also identifies the enablers and barriers in the adoption process. Despite this the main challenges faced by the rural marketers are listed as below:

- Infrastructural problems
- Limited financial resources
- Limited technology
- Orthodox cultures and beliefs
- Limited media availability
- Limited marketing facilities collaboration between systems.
- Lack of awareness and understanding
- Limited Government support.

Opportunities in Rural Communications

While there are challenges in rural communication, there are opportunities also for social marketing efforts which include:

- The tight-knit social network that understands each other well
- The commonality of the word of mouth communications
- Strong informal communications networks
- Government Agencies that are willing to partner with rural marketers, such as the Cooperative Extension System
- Community leaders are easily identifiable because of smaller groups
- Consumers changing preferences towards traditional products.
- Availability of Media coverage because of lower competition.

Role of IT

- Information technology facilitates access to information.
- IT helps inaccurate forecasting of weather conditions and market dynamics.
- Help in promoting government schemes for the benefit of rural marketers.
- IT helps in providing better services to the consumers and speedy claim services.
- Monitoring & tracking of product performance and feedback.
- IT ensures better interaction between the company and the consumer.
- Correct feedback helps in the improvement of the product.
- IT helps in cost reduction on distribution and transportation.
- Cost-effective, doorstep delivery is possible due to the use of information technology.
- IT helps in the Development of customer Databases.
- IT helps in developing customized products for the different target segments with effective tracking.

Types of E-Commerce

1. Business to Business (B2B)
2. Business to Consumer (B2C)
3. Business to Government (B2G)
4. Consumer to Consumer (C2C)

5. Government to Consumer (G2C)
6. Government to Business (G2B)

Importance of ICT

E-commerce in the recent years has transformed the way businesses are carried in and around the world. Agriculture has also been impacted by the E-commerce and has found its way in agriculture. E- commerce has many applications which can be helpful in agricultural activities'-commerce requires that both buyers and sellers have access to the Internet and that they are able to use the required software's. Common agribusiness B2B transactions such as buying, selling, trading etc can use ecommerce for increasing efficiency. In B2C categories also e-commerce can be used for activities such as, Remote Service, and Maintenance referred to as Agri business to Agri business (A2A) and Agri business to grower (A2G). Other benefits of ecommerce in agriculture can be identified as follows:

Promotion of Information Flow

The exchange of relevant information about agricultural products, availability, their characteristics, advantages, disadvantages, etc., can be increased through the use of information on the Internet during ecommerce transactions. Internet technology also acts as an important link between farmers in the food production irrespective of their geographic location. This increase market access through online transactions and reduces geographic obstacles, such as time and distance.

Market and Price Transparency

Online transactions allow comparison of products on pricing which increases transparency in the transactions. Price differentials due to geographic location can be minimized because of competition. This benefits farmers in terms of uniform prices with regard to input prices. This may be more relevant where many existing products are not differentiated on a regular basis.

Reduction in Transaction Costs

With the application of ecommerce, many transactions through the supply chain are either eliminated or simplified. In this way, transaction costs are drastically reduced or even eliminated.

Increase in Online Cooperatives

The processes of ecommerce transactions give emergence to new opportunities for furthering the concept of cooperatives. From the perspective of farmers, e-cooperatives provide a solution for small businesses.

Reduce dominance of Middlemen

E-Commerce presents an advantage to both consumers and sellers. E-commerce eliminates the middlemen and inventory reduction which makes it easy for a seller to pass on the benefits to consumers at a lower price. Agri-marketing can benefit immensely from e-commerce both in B2B and B2C markets. While e-NAM is the government driven government which has promoted private players such as Big Basket to fill the gap of the B2C market through policy initiatives like direct purchase and e- trading.

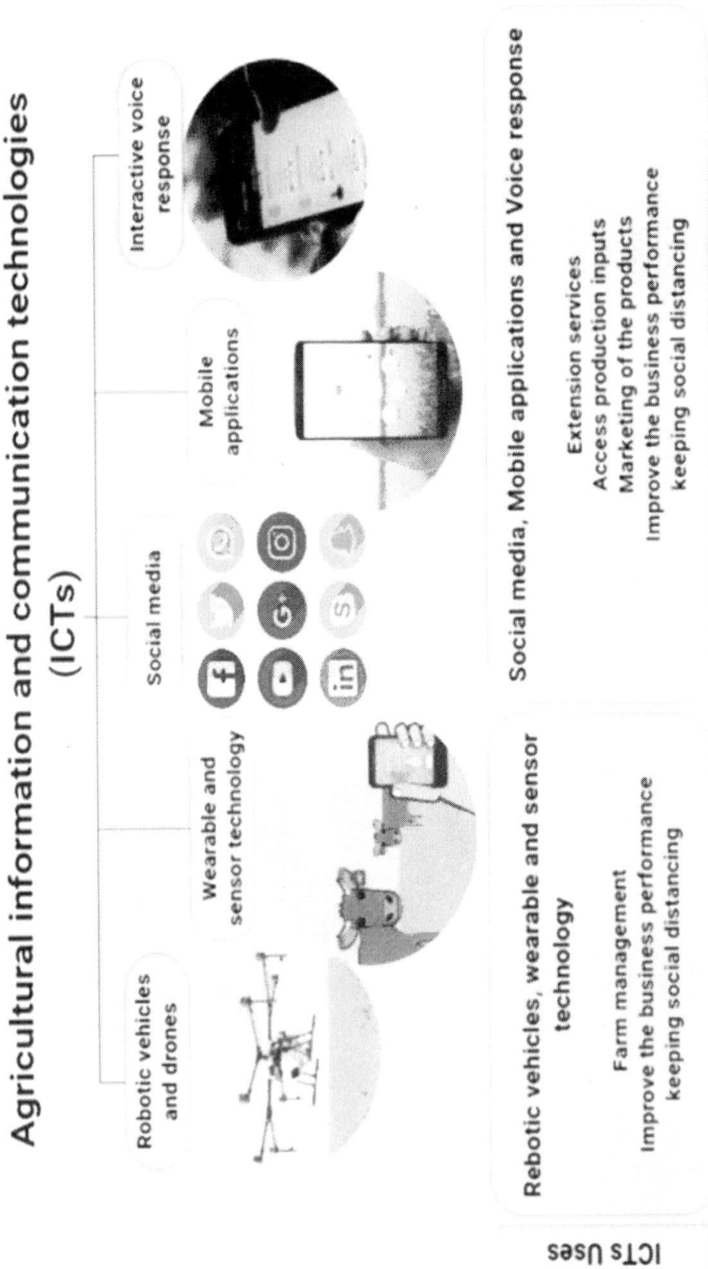

ICT as a Key for Rural Development
Source: Researchgate

The use of ICT (Information and Communication Technology) increases the effectiveness of distribution systems for rural marketing. The government of India has realized this fact and it is because of this reason that it had taken many initiatives related to ICT for the development of the rural markets. A good number of projects are already under progress for the development of rural markets and many more are going to be implemented in the coming days. As per NCAER (National Council for Applied Economic Research), the number of rural households in India is expected to grow from 111 Million to 210 Million by the end of the year 2021 as compared to Urban India.

The use of ICT in rural distribution strategies may be related to:

- Usage of proper logistics and supply chain system
- Creating Joint distribution systems
- Creating Feeder towns for further Distribution.
- Use of Mandis, Rural Haats and fairs.
- E-Commerce and Private Courier services.
- Partnership with Marketing agencies and NGO's
- Use of Internet, Intranet and Extranet
- Creating infrastructure for Rural Malls.

To conclude we can say that ICT has a diverse role to play in the development of rural markets.ICT holds the key to rural development. Efforts should be made to increase the usage of ICT in rural areas by creating awareness about the advantages of using ICT and how its usage can lead to the development of the rural markets and the distribution systems thus, having a substantial impact on the economy of the rural area. The government should also invest in the infrastructural developments of rural India along with the technological and financial investors, because without the development in the areas of electricity, communication media, transportation etc.ICT cannot be effectively implemented. The awareness of the rural marketers towards ICT can increase the productivity of the rural products which would enhance the economical growth of the country.

Tools for ICT: eNAM and AGMARKNET

Electronic National Agriculture Market (eNAM) is a pan-India initiative by the government of India which is an electronic trading portal which networks the APMC mandis to build create a unified market for agricultural commodities nationally. National agriculture market network seeks to regulate the wholesale market (known as the APMC market) through a virtual platform. National Agriculture Market provides better marketing opportunities for the farmers to promote their products and sell their products through online portals in a competitive and transparent price discovery system. The online payment facility commensurate with the quality of the products is also available under e-NAM initiative. The eNAM Portal provides a single-window for all APMC related information. e-NAM includes the arrivals of the products & prices, available offers and discounts on the products, among other services.E- NAM is instrumental in reducing transaction costs and information non-uniformity. Each state in India has its agricultural market areas, which is administered by the Agricultural Produce Marketing Committee (APMC) imposing its marketing regulation and fees. The different policies of different states levying different fees end up in inflating the prices of the rural marketer, which does not benefit the marketer. These issues are effectively addressed by National Agriculture Market by creating a unified market through an online trading platform, both, at State and National level which promotes uniformity, across the integrated markets, mitigates the no uniformity between buyers and sellers, based on actual demand and supply of the products.

Objectives of e-NAM

The objective of e-NAM is to create a national e-market platform for transparent transactions and uniform prices in the regulated markets. The states make suitable provisions in their APMC Act for promotion of e-trading by Agricultural Produce Marketing Committee (APMC).

- It's a national e-market platform for transparent sale transactions and price discovery.
- Liberal licensing of traders, buyers and commission agents by State authorities without any pre- condition of physical presence.
- One license for a trader/buyer which is valid across all markets in the State.
- Uniformity of quality standards in every market to enable informed bidding by buyers.
- Single point for levying market fees.
- Provision of Soil Testing Laboratories near the selected mandi to facilitate visiting farmers to access this facility in the mandi itself. It has a provision of a strategic partner which customizes the specific requirements of the mandis in the States.

Small Farmers Agribusiness Consortium (SFAC) is the lead agency for implementing eNAM under the aegis of the Ministry of Agriculture and Farmers' Welfare, Government of India the Strategic Partner M/s. Nagarjuna Fertilizers and Chemicals Ltd. The strategic partner is responsible for the development, operation and maintenance of the platform. The broad role of the Strategic Partner is meeting the specific requirements of the mandis in the States who are willing to integrate with the National Agriculture Market.

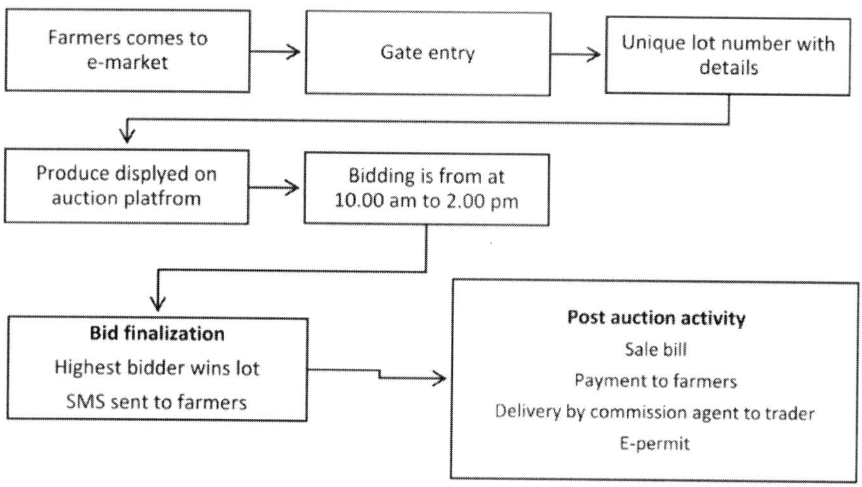

Process flowchart of e-Market
Source: Reddy, (2018)

From a system of undercover auctions in some mandis to the automation of these activities, the entire process has come a long way. The benefit of eNAM comes from computerized weighing machines linked to the eNAM portal through Bluetooth. There were initial hiccups at the beginning which were poor internet connectivity, software glitches and problems in online payments. Many of these problems have been solved by the Small Farmers Agribusiness Consortium (SFAC), an autonomous entity promoted by the Agriculture Ministry), the implementing agency for eNAM.

Advantages of eNAM

- The advantage of eNAM is in a reduction in bookkeeping and reporting system which is now generated automatically.
- Better monitoring and regulation of traders and agents.
- Complete transparency in systems which eliminate manipulation of tendering and auctioning process.

- Improvement in the fee collection by all the transactions taking place in the market.
- Reduction in manpower requirements as technology is used for the processes.
- Analysis and forecasting of the arrivals and prices.
- Availability of all the information on the website directly.
- The biggest achievement of eNAM is automated bidding.
- Faster flow of information such as SMS alerts are sent to the farmers for updates.

Agricultural Marketing Network

Agricultural Marketing Information Network (AGMARKNET) was launched in March 2000 by the Union Ministry of Agriculture. It is used for effective information exchange. The portal of AGMARKNET is maintained by National Informatics Centre (NIC). It provides information related to facilitates generation and transmission of prices, commodity arrival, dissemination of information to producers, consumers, traders, transparently and quickly. The AGMARKNET is an e-governance portal that caters to the requirements of farmers, industry, policymakers and academic institutions by providing all the information related to agricultural marketing in a single window. The portal helped those farmers who do not have sufficient resources to get adequate market information. AGMARKNET facilitates web- based information flow onthe daily arrivals and prices of agricultural produce markets spread across the country. The information on the AGMARKNET portal is available in 8 regional languages and English. It displays the information of wholesale markets Commodity wise, Variety wise daily prices and arrivals information. The AGMARKNET portal has a database of about 300 commodities and 2,000 varieties. The database developed under AGMARKNET would also be linked to other agricultural databases, for instance, on area, production, the yield of crops, land use, cost of cultivation, agriculture exports and imports, and so on, to evolve a data warehouse. This would provide a sound base for planning demand is driven agriculture production. AGMARKNET is also expected to play a crucial role in enabling e- commerce in agricultural marketing.

Objectives of AGMARKNET

- To promote the creation of agricultural marketing infrastructure by providing information to State, cooperative and private sector investments.
- To promote the creation of scientific information and to promote financing to increase farmers' income.
- To promote Integrated Value Chains to provide vertical integration of farmers with primary processors.
- To use ICT as a vehicle to make the rural marketers about the challenges and how to respond to these new challenges in agricultural marketing.
- To create a nationwide information network system for speedy collection and dissemination of market information for timely utilization by farmers.
- To support quality certification of agricultural commodities for better prices for their graded produce.
- To facilitate private investment in setting up of agribusiness projects for the assured market to producers and strengthen linkages with producers and their groups.
- To undertake and promote training, research, education, and consultancy in the Agri marketing sector.

To conclude the information provided through the AGMARKNET portal includes:

- Prices and Arrivals and future trends
- Grades and Standards
- Commodity Profiling
- Market Profiling
- Other Reports
- Research Studies
- Companies involved in Contract Farming
- Government Schemes of DMI for strengthening Marketing Infrastructure

This portal helps in creating uniformity in agricultural prices and thus is of immense use for the rural marketers and the stakeholders.

6

Rural Marketing Research

Market Research

The market research process is equally critical to rural marketing as to urban marketing because of two main reasons:

- The marketer has a limited understanding of the rural/urban consumer
- The marketer who is urban-oriented may need to find different ways to understand the decision variables in the urban market.

This requires the use of research methodology methods that are best suited for understanding the rural markets. The main challenge in the rural market is the non-availability of secondary data which leads to an inadequate sampling framework. The availability of secondary data can be generated by:

- Census or the National Sample Survey giving income-wise breakup of population.
- Providing separate data for industrial products;
- The questionnaire should be different languages that can be understood by rural consumers.

Marketing Research Objectives

The main objectives of the market research process for the marketer are to understand the market conditions, the market segments, consumer preferences and the situation of demand and supply. It is essential to understand the objectives before a market research process is initiated. The correctness of the objectives would define the accuracy of the market research findings. The main objectives of the market research process are as follows:

- Demand forecasting for the product for one year or more.
- Demand forecasting takes into consideration the past data market dynamics and changing marketing conditions.
- Identification of enablers and barriers for the product.

- Market share of competitive companies
- Brand equity and positions of competing Brands.
- Competitive prices with regards to brand equity.
- The requirement for the advertisements and promotional activities.

From the consumer's perspective the marketing research objectives are as follows:

- The needs, wants and benefits which the consumer is seeking from the product.
- Frequency of product usage.
- Brand Recall.
- Consumer Perceptions about price and Brand
- Consumer decision making and people involved in decision making.
- Reasons for brand preferences.

There are different types of Marketing Research processes which are used in the study by different research agencies and the companies, but some of the most commonly used methods for carrying out research are as follows:

- Exploratory research is conducted to find something which has not been studied until now. It is exploring something which can be thought of or an idea. These researches are in the new areas to find out something novel. In the marketing studies, this type of research is used to develop some new product concept, an idea or service.
- Statistical research helps in finding the frequency of events like product usage or repeat purchases. In this type of study, the variables are already decided and the study is conducted to find out the impact of one variable over another. Statistical researches are useful for analyzing quantitatively using software like SPSS.
- Casual research means cause and effect studies. The causal studies analyses the cause and how the market would respond to this cause. For example: To find the effect of price rise on the sale of the product.

Market Survey

Market Survey is used for the collection of data with the help of an instrument called a Questionnaire. The data is collected directly from the respondents. The market survey can be an expensive process that involves considerable time and effort. It is therefore advisable to carry out a sample survey in a limited area on a limited sample to test the validity and reliability of the instrument. The market surveys can be used in both the Qualitative and Quantitative market research methods. There are various methods to conduct market surveys. The most common methods used for market survey are explained below:

Observation Method

The observation method is used in closed conditions like classrooms, office space, etc. to get the real information regarding the usage of the product. In some cases, the researcher uses simulation methods to understand the problems in simulated conditions. For example Use of CCTVs, Sensors and smoke detectors to know about the various parameters.

Personal Interviews

In personal interviews, the researcher meets the respondent personally to collect first-hand relevant information with the help of a structured or unstructured questionnaire. The data collected is extrapolated for the entire sample to carry out the analysis. The personal interviews are time-consuming because of the dependability on the interviewee and are expensive, but the data collected is more reliable and accurate.

Mail Surveys

The mail surveys are conducted by sending the questionnaire to the respondent and return them to the researcher. Mail surveys are a cheap method for data collection, but the main problem with this method is that the respondent does not take the pain to fill the questionnaire and then post it back to the researcher. The data collected may not be reliable. Telephone surveys mean collecting data through telephones but the problem with this method is that the respondent replying to the call may not be the right person.

Marketing Research Methods

There are two basic methods of doing Marketing Research

1. Primary Research

- The sources of primary data are questionnaire.
- Delphi method (expert opinions)

2. Secondary research

Sources of secondary data are as follows:

- The firm's internal source, include P/L Statements, previous MR Reports.
- Staff members coming from competitive firms.
- Government publications and notifications from Directorate of audiovisual publicity,
- Research organizations.
- Trade publications, Magazines, etc and every possible area of business are in the market.
- Competitors balance sheets.
- Publications by associations like FICCI, CII and ASSOCHAM.
- Newspapers and magazines like financial times, Business Today, Business India.
- Market Research Organizations, like ORG-Marg, who sell MR Reports at a price.
- Publications by Reserve Bank of India and Financial Institutions like IDBI, ICICI, and UTI, etc.
- Foreign Government Data, International publications
- Published Documents

Secondary data is the data for which somebody else has collected as Primary data.

Steps in the Market Research Process

The main steps in the market research process are:

1. Problem definition
2. Selection of the survey method
3. Sampling
4. Questionnaire development
5. Pilot survey
6. Selection of investigators
7. Collection of data
8. Analysis of data.
9. Tabulating

10. Interpreting data
11. Summarizing findings and recommendations
12. Report writing
13. Recommendation and Follow up

The above process can be diagrammatically represented as given below. The following diagram

represents the important points which are part of an important part of a marketing research process:

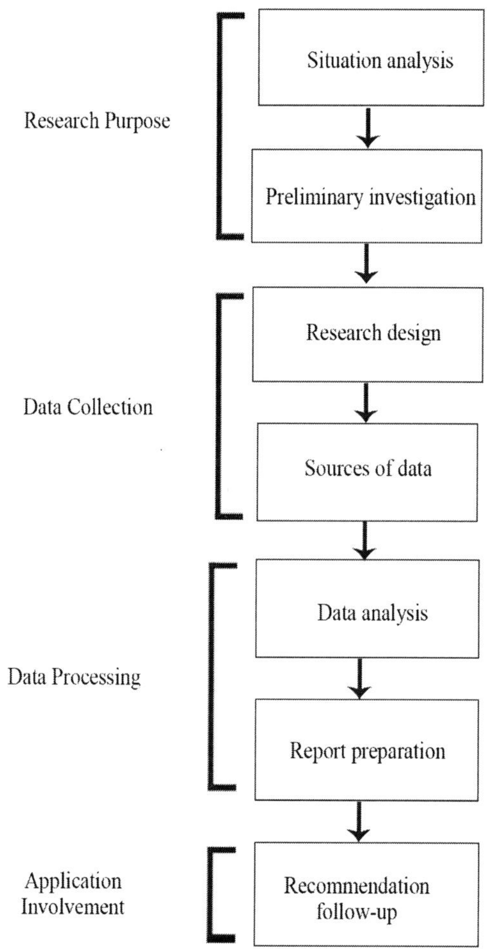

Fig. 6.1: Marketing Research Process Design flow
Source: Panda et.al, (2015)

Components of Rural Marketing Information System:

Rural Marketing Information System can be divided into three parts. They are as follows:

a. Market Research

b. Market and Sales Reports

c. Marketing Intelligence

Market Research

A study of the size of the market demand depends on customer and user preferences and the social and economic factors affecting the nature of the market. Market research is useful for:

- Estimating demand and market share.
- Identification of Target segments
- sales forecasting; and
- Measurement of sales forces' effectiveness.

Market and Sales Report

Any future decision depends on past trends and data. The market expansion also depends upon past market trends and sales reports. Reports must be classified as timely under different headings. The value of a market report to interested parties like producers, manufacturers, and others not only depends on the swiftness with which it is gathered but is also dependent on its accuracy and correct interpretation. Market and sales and necessary:

- To measure sales performance against targets and within budgets
- To study past trends of sales and customers behaviours; and
- To adapt sales operation on a short term

Market Intelligence

It is pertinent for the marketer to know where and when a product should be distributed for sale, which is the best mode of transportation for distribution of the product which is efficient and efficient. In India the information of the rural marketing is collected and disseminated through:

- Traders and business organizations that send their agents in the markets to gather data which is normally confidential and for their personal use. Their reliance on other sources of information is very little.

- Journals, newspapers, and other print and non-print media. There is considerable scope for improvement in the supply of market news to the trade, manufacturers, and rural marketers.

Such information is generally not available except in the case of essential commodities like wheat, rice, groundnut, cotton, etc. For a rural marketer to bargain for the proper price of his produce, he must be posted with information regarding the prices in different markets. Presently the rural marketer has no reliable source through relevant information that can be sought. Some information is published by the government regarding trade, production and prices, but the information is published is not timely and is of practically no use to the rural marketer. The information regarding the prices is also lost largely due to the reason that different markets quote prices for different units of weight, and without reference to quality. But now due to the latest technologies, it has become much easier. Now a day it is common to see rural marketers and traders moving with mobile phones in hand operating with support infrastructure such as transportation, godowns, etc. The scenario has much changed. While designing a rural management information system, it is important to ensure that the data collected is relevant, reliable, complete, consistent, and timely. These parameters should also be checked while disseminating information out of such a rural management information system.

Sources of Rural Credit

The rural sector plays an important role in the economic development of a country. India also being a developing country depends largely on the rural sector but the issue of access to rural credit remains a critical problem. This section focuses on the characteristics of rural credit markets and the sources of rural credit available in India. Access to the credit has an impact on the output production, household income, and poverty reduction. The financial institutions must expand their target clients and capital allocation and the government should ensure that market competitiveness is maintained in the long run. There are overlaps in three terms and some circles are used interchangeably like "rural credit", "agriculture credit", and "microcredit" in financial sectors. The basic difference the three is this that rural credit refers to credit services in rural areas that aim at people at different income level, while agriculture credit is primarily for the agriculture-related activities.

Financial institutions also offer credits for urban agriculture which are part of the credit for urban agriculture activities which are growing plants and the raising of animals around cities. And lastly, the Microfinance is the provision of financial services to poor and low-income people, by which they finance their activities to generate income, build assets, smooth consumption, and risk management. Financial services not only include credit products (micro-credit), but also savings, money transfers, and insurance.

Rural economic growth depends on the funds on a seasonal basis due to the productivity of different crops in different seasons. The gap between sowing a seed and harvesting and finally revenue generation is fairly long for this reason the rural producers depend on the credits from various government agencies to fulfill the requirements of fertilizers, seeds and personal expenses. Before independence moneylenders exploited the peasants and landless workers by lending money on huge-interest rates.

To solve this problem of the farmers the Indian government started social banking that provided funds to rural producers to satisfy the requirements of rural credit. In the year 1982, National Bank for Agriculture and Rural Development (NABARD) was formed as an apex body to regulate and provide all the financial services related to the rural economy. Further, the Green Revolution changed the credit system of the country, resulting in a better system for rural credit. In the current scenario, rural banking includes a set of various financial institutions, like regional rural banks (RRBs), cooperatives, commercial banks, Self-Help groups, and land development banks. They provide credit to rural producers at cheaper interest rates.

Some of the major credit sources of rural credit in India are as follows:

• Co-operative Credit Societies

This is the most economical source of rural credit. It was set up to facilitate the complete credit needs for small and medium farmers. Co-operative Credit Societies increased their network in India soon after its few years for inception. They started assisting rural producers with short-term loans issued by Credit Societies (PACs). But due to limited financial liquidity, the co-operatives could not meet all the credit requirements so the money lenders kept on controlling the rural economic markets, such as District cooperative Banks.

• Land Development Bank

This type of credit is called a land mortgage. It provides rural producers with a long-term loan option upon the mortgage of their land for a period of 15 to 20 years at low-interest rates. These types of loans are taken if the rural producers have some land developments work or digging of wells, etc. But due to the lack of awareness of such banks they met limited success even then the land development bank has made notable progress, However, such a credit system grew increasingly immensely due to the active support of the government and financial institutions over the years.

• Commercial Banks

The commercial banks earlier used to collect funds deposited by the urban consumer and then dispersed these funds to the rural producers in the form of loans to fulfil their credit requirements. Initially, the commercial banks neglected agriculture and rural industries because by agriculture was considered as low return on investment and high-risk venture. But now the commercial banks provide both direct and indirect loans to agriculture. Direct finance is issued for small and medium- term and indirect finance is given in the advance form to purchase things like grains and fertilizers. Commercial banks also provided credit to government agencies like the Food Corporation of India, and State food agencies for activities like food procurement. The State Bank of India initiated the 'village adoption scheme' to examine the credit requirements of the farmers.

• Regional Rural Banks

The government established regional rural banks to examine the specific needs of landless workers, small and marginal farmers and rural poor. The regional rural banks focused specifically on the need of the rural population only.

• The Government

In case of an emergency like earthquakes, floods and famine the Government of India provide short and long term loans to farmers if there is an emergency like famine and flood. These types of loans are also known as Taccavi loans. Under this system of rural financing, the Government provides advance loans at a reasonably low rate of interest to the rural producers for any other purposes related to agriculture. But due to the inadequacy of funds and low recovery rate, it failed to attract the farmers. These Taccavi loans were introduced to enhance productivity and help poor farmers to increase their income.

• (NBFC's) Non-Banking Financial Companies

The NBFC's also constitute an important source of credit financing. The NBFC's are preferred by rural producers because they charge a substantially higher rate of interest than the market rates.

• Credit Unions

A credit union is a voluntary association of rural producers who save their money together and provide loans to each other in times of need at a relatively lower rate of interest. These are caller co-operative credit societies. They are nonprofit bodies which are also called low-cost credit institutions. Most credit unions also provide the borrower with "free" credit life insurance.

• Microfinance

The microfinance institutions have caught the attention of the policymakers in India. The fundamental premise of providing microfinance services is participation in entrepreneurial activities to improve the economic conditions of poor. Microfinance plays an important role in the economic development of a country. Microfinance, which is also referred to as microcredit is a type of banking service provided to poor or low-income individuals who have no other access to financial services. Microfinance is an effective tool for reducing poverty and empowering poor people to make them financially independent.. Microfinance is about offering a wide range of financial services like credit, insurance, financial, non-financial and networking services and deposit services to a poor and low- income individual who cannot access conventional financial services for lack of collateral. The Micro financial institutions play an important role in empowerment of the poor peoples.

• Local Landlords

The local landlords are big landholders who operate as lenders in villages and provide credit to the poor villagers on exorbitant interest rates. A local landlord gives credit to a worker and also regularly rents land to him when he is need of money. The system of availing loans from local landlords is still prevalent in India despite numerous schemes by the banks and the presence of micro financial institutions.

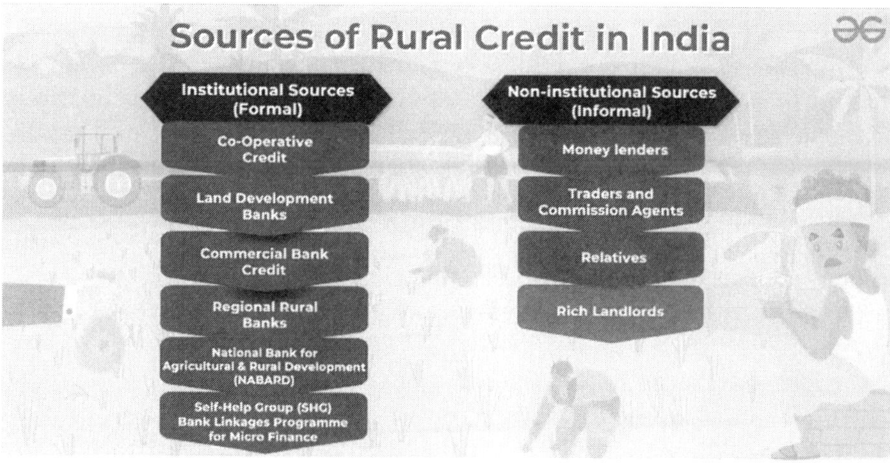

Fig. 6.2: Organization and Institutional Structure of Agricultural Credit India
Source: Shivam Panda

Other Types of Consumer Credit

- **Revolving credit:** It is a credit arrangement in which the financier grants credit on a revolving basis. The consumer is entitled to avail credit to the extent sanctioned as credit limit ex: Krishi Credit Card or Agriculture credit cards.
- **Fixed credit**: it is like a term loan where the financier provides loans for a fixed period. The credit has to be repaid within a stipulated period for example monthly installment loan, hire purchase, EMIs.
- **Cash Loan**: Under this type of credit banks and financial institutions provide money with which the rural producer's types of equipment for personal/Agricultural consumption. In the case of Cash loans, the lender and seller are different and the lender does not have any responsibility of the seller.
- **Secured Finance**: when the credit provided by the financial institutions is secured by collateral it is called secured finance. The collateral can be land papers, real property or any asset, etc. to satisfy the debt in the event of default by the borrower.
- **Unsecured Finance**: When there is no collateral or security given by the consumer against which money is granted by financial institutions, it is called unsecured finance. It is a risky type of financing.

Regulatory Bodies in Rural Development (NABARD)

NABARD is a Government of India body that came into existence on 12 July 1982 by transferring the agricultural credit functions of Reserve Bank of India and refinance functions of the then Agricultural Refinance and Development Corporation (ARDC). NABARD was dedicated to the service of the nation on 05 November 1982 with an initial capital of ₹100 crore. Its paid-up capital stood at ₹12, 580 crores as of 31 March 2019. After the recomposition of share capital between the Government of India and RBI, Although the genesis of NABARD was to help the rural farmers and the rural population engaged in farm businesses the schemes of NABARD were enjoyed by the rich also. The rich traders use the credit facilities of NABARD and give loans to the poor at higher interest. Thus the rural traders and money lenders earned easy money with bankers' investments. The role of the NABARD role in rural development has been phenomenal. National Bank for Agriculture &Rural Development facilitates credit flow for promotion and development of agriculture, cottage, and village industries. The importance of institutional credit in boosting the rural economy has been clear to the Government right from the planning stage. It was for this reason that the Reserve Bank of India (RBI) at the insistence of the Government of India, constituted a Committee to Review the Arrangements for Institutional Credit for Agriculture and Rural Development (CRAFICARD) to look into the financial problems of the rural producers.

NABARD aims at building an empowering rural India through specific goal-oriented departments which can be categorized broadly into three heads which are as follows:

- Financial
- Developmental
- Supervision

Through these above-mentioned initiatives, NABARB touches almost every aspect of the rural economy. From providing financial support to build rural infrastructure to preparing district level credit plans to guide and motivating the banking industry in achieving these targets. In the supervisory role, NABARD supervises the working of Cooperative Banks and Regional Rural Banks (RRBs) and helps them in developing sound banking practices and providing them facilities to move to the CBS platform. NABARD also helps in designing new development schemes from training handicraft artisans to providing them with a marketing platform for marketing and selling of these articles.

Functions of NABARD Credit Functions

- Framing policy and guidelines for rural financial institutions.
- Providing credit facilities.
- Monitoring the flow of ground-level rural credit.
- Preparation of credit plans annually for all districts for identification of credit potential.

Development Functions

- Help cooperative banks and Regional Rural Banks to prepare their development actions plans
- Help Regional Rural Banks and the sponsor banks to enter into MoUs with state governments and cooperative banks to improve the affairs of the Regional Rural Banks.
- Monitor the implementation of development action plans of banks.
- Provide financial support for the training institutes of cooperative banks, commercial banks, and Regional Rural Banks.
- Provide financial assistance to cooperative banks for building improved management information systems, computerization of operations and development of human resources.

Supervisory Functions

- Undertakes inspection of Regional Rural Banks (RRBs) and Cooperative Banks (other than urban/primary cooperative banks).
- Undertakes inspection of State Cooperative Agriculture and Rural Development Banks (SCARDBs) and apex noncredit cooperative.
- Provides recommendations to Reserve Bank of India on the issue of licenses to Cooperative Banks, opening of new branches by State Cooperative Banks and Regional Rural Banks (RRBs).
- Undertakes portfolio inspections besides offsite surveillance of Cooperative Banks and Regional Rural Banks (RRBs).

Some of the important initiatives taken by NABARD to help the rural population in facilitating the requirements of funds are:

a) Producers Organization Development Fund (PODF)

NABARD has taken an initiative for supporting producer organizations in adopting a flexible approach to meet the needs of producers. To give a special focus, the "Producers Organization Development Fund" (PODF) has been set up w.e.f. 01 April 2011, with an initial corpus of ₹ 50 crore. Any registered producer organization or Producers Company (as defined under Sec. 581 A in part IXA of Company's Act, 1956), Producers Cooperatives, registered Farmer Federations, MACS (Mutually aided cooperative society), industrial cooperative societies, other registered federations, PACS, etc. set up by producers are eligible from the Fund.

Support under PODF is provided as under:

- Support in the form of grant is available for promotion, capacity building & market interventions.
- As most of the producer organizations are having a low capital base, the scope for NABARD's intervention under PODF has been enhanced to support them for contributing to share capital.

b) Tribal Development Program

NABARD has been closely associated with tribal development and sustainable livelihoods through orchard based farming systems. As an integral component of NABARD's Natural Resource Management (NRM) policy of providing sustainable livelihoods, NABARD provided support for the holistic development of tribal communities with orchard establishment as the core element.

Based on the successful experience of this Program, NABARD embarked upon an ambitious program of replicating the wadi model across the country. In this direction, NABARD created a Tribal Development Fund (TDF) with a corpus of ₹ 50 crore, out of its profits for 2003-04. The corpus was augmented from time to time. All projects under TDF are implemented by partnering with State Governments, the Government of India, NGOs, and Corporates.

c) Watershed Development Programme

In the budget speech of 1999-2000, the creation of a Watershed Development Fund (WDF) in the National Bank for Agriculture and Rural Development (NABARD) with broad objectives of unification of multiplicity of watershed development programs into a single national initiative through the involvement of village-level institutions and PFAs was announced. As per the budget speech, the watershed development program was created in NABARD with a contribution of Rs. 100 crore each by the Ministry of Agriculture, Government of India (GoI) and NABARD.

d) Climate Change Adaptation and Mitigation

Designing policies for Natural Resources Management and & climate change adaptation and mitigation

- Functional role as National Implementation Entity (NIE) for Adaptation Fund through Adaptation Fund Board (AFB) for Climate Change Adaptation (CCA) Projects
- Implementation & monitoring of projects approved by the Adaptation Fund Board
- Training and capacity building of stakeholders
- Collaboration with other national and international agencies like Ministry of Environment and Forests (MoEF, GoI), Global Environment Fund (GEF), Green Climate Fund / for accreditation, etc. and up scaling of Climate change adaptation and monitoring and pilot projects on climate proofing of watershed projects under WDF

e) Scheme for setting up of Agri-clinic and Agribusiness centres

A scheme for financing agriculture graduates to set up agri-clinics and agribusiness centres was launched in 2001-02 with an aim at supplementing the existing Extension Network. The objective of this scheme was to accelerate the process of technology transfer to agriculture and assist the efforts of State agencies in providing inputs and other services to the rural producers. The salient features of the scheme are as under:

- The scheme is open to agriculture graduates and postgraduates in agriculture or allied subjects.
- The outer ceiling of the project cost is ₹ 10 lakh for individuals and 40 lakhs for groups.
- Margin money assistance from NABARD's Soft Loan Assistance Fund up to 50 per cent of the margin prescribed by banks to meet any shortfall in the borrower's contribution.

The National Bank has prepared Model Project Profiles related to few activities indicating the estimated cost and income streams. The banks have the freedom to select the borrower's entrepreneurs and the activity depending on the potential of the area subject to technical feasibility and the financial viability of the proposals. The scheme has been launched for creating entrepreneurs in the area of agribusiness so that rural graduates become job givers rather than job seekers. Since the government has launched several programs for entrepreneurship development therefore this scheme has been shadowed by the new better and lucrative schemes.

Corporate Social Responsibility in Rural Marketing

Corporate social responsibility is traditionally seen as a philanthropic activity. The companies' act of 2013 introduced the idea of corporate social responsibility for mandatory disclosure, promoting greater transparency and disclosure. Ministry of corporate affairs has recently notified section 135 and schedule VII of the companies act as well as the provisions of the companies (corporate social responsibility), Rules, 2014 (CSR Rules) which has come into effect from 1st April, 2014.The beginning of the 21st century in India has seen the term corporate social responsibility coming to the forefront of the development of discussion. The present government has made it mandatory that every company has to contribute at least 2 per cent of their net profits on corporate social responsibility activities. Therefore in recent times, Corporate Social Responsibility is emerging as an important concept of business philosophy, reflecting the impact of business on society in the context of sustainable development. The concept of corporate social responsibility focuses on the responsibility of the company towards its, employees, creditors, suppliers, government, and community and not only on the maximization of profit for shareholders. Corporate social responsibility not only includes corporate regulatory compliance but also focuses on the act of making a business successful through taking due care of environmental and social issues in a way that is helpful to the planet earth. Many studies conducted on CSR and rural development in India help understand the behaviour of rural producers in the emerging markets. "CSR means Making Good Business Sense". According to Holme and Watts "Corporate Social Responsibility is the continuing commitment by business to behave ethically and contribute to economic development while improving the quality of life of the workforce and their families as well as of the local community and society at large". Although there is no single universally accepted definition of corporate social responsibility, it has generally come to mean business decision making linked to ethical values, legal compliance, and respect for people, community, and environment. Indian rural companies are expected to discharge their stakeholder responsibilities and societal obligations, along with their shareholder- wealth maximization goal.

Corporate social responsibility (CSR) is the responsibility recognized by the companies for acting in a socially responsible manner. All the leading companies in India are involved in corporate social responsibility (CSR) programs in areas like education, health, livelihood creation, skill development, and empowerment of weaker sections of the society. Some of the notable companies are the Tata Group, Infosys, Bharti Enterprises, ITC Welcome Group, and Indian Oil Corporation among others. Some of the main activities of the companies which the company needs to follow are to treat employees fairly and with respect and providing them fair remuneration, Operate with integrity and in an ethical manner in all its business dealings with a customer, suppliers, lenders, and Respect human rights, Sustain the environment for future generations and be a responsible neighbor in the community and a good corporate citizen. Because of the above, it is important to study and understand how corporate enterprises are using corporate social responsibility initiatives. The benefits of corporate social responsibility to rural development can be enlisted as follows:

- Win new business.
- Increase customer loyalty and retention.
- Develop and enhance relationships with customers, suppliers, and networks.
- Attract, retain and maintain a satisfied workforce and be an employee-friendly organization.
- Save money on energy and operating costs and risk management.
- Differentiate yourself from your competitors.
- Innovation and enhancing companies' influence
- Improve the brand equity of the company.
- Provide access to investment and funding opportunities.

In the present scenario corporate social responsibility is a new and widely used concept in which companies voluntarily contribute to a better society and a cleaner environment. It was initially voluntary but since most of the Indian companies were not contributing to CSR activities the government of India made it mandatory for the companies to contribute at least 2 per cent of their net profits on CSR activities. Apart from contributing to societal welfare, the companies should also act responsibly towards the environment. CSR has been making a prominent impact on the Indian social system by supplementing development projects for social well being. Corporate social responsibility is not a new concept for India its roots can be traced back to the Vedic times. Apart from the private and government companies other public organizations like the Banking Sector are growing larger and powerful in their contribution towards CSR activities. Various Non-government organizations put pressure on Banks to act responsibly towards their stakeholders.

Corporate Social Responsibility
Section 135 of the companies Act, 2013
COMPANY

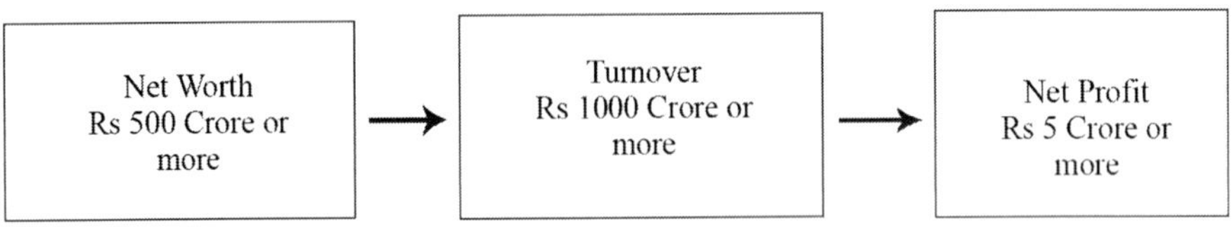

CSR can be defined as companies' responsibility towards the community and environment in which it operates. Companies can fulfill this responsibility through waste and pollution reduction and by contributing to the environment, educational and social programs, and by undertaking similar activities. CSR is not charity or mere donations. In CSR corporate entities contributes towards the social good. Socially responsible companies do not only exploit resources that increase only their profits. They use CSR to integrate economic, environmental and social objectives with the company's operations and growth. CSR activities help in brand building of a company's among its customers and society.

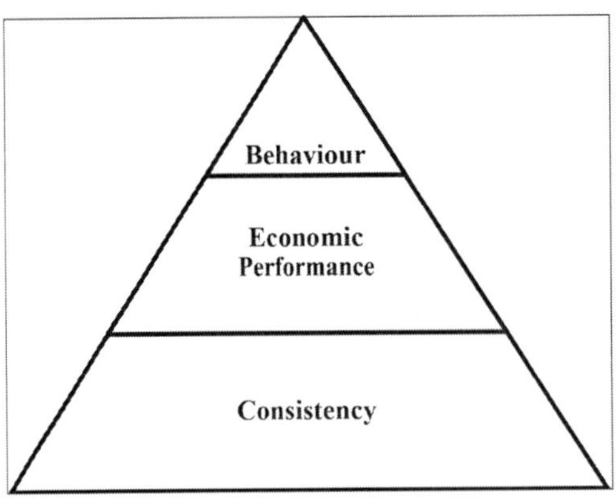

CSR Models: Corporate citizenship Model

Fig. 6.3: The Pyramid of Corporate Social Responsibility
Source: (Carroll, 2012)

To be a corporate citizen a corporate has to satisfy four conditions:

1. Consistently satisfactory
2. Sustainable economic performance
3. Ethical actions
4. Behaviour

A particular firm's commitment to corporate citizenship requires the fulfillment of certain social responsibility. The concept of corporate social responsibility (CSR) is on the top agenda of policymakers, managers and social activists in recent times. It is because of the emerging legislation on corporate governance, the compulsory minimum number of non-executive directors, and disclosure of far more details of the operations and finances of an enterprise. The critical issues in CSR would be around the definition of the boundaries on the extent of the activities, setting of standards, as well as the scope and limitation for voluntary action. The fact is that discharging social responsibilities beyond and outside the business processes involved directly in the operations adds significantly to costs. Some industrial groups such as the Tatas, the founder of the TATA group sir JRD Tata was personally enthusiastic about all aspects of labour welfare, including family planning in pre-independence India. The Group introduced the concept of the minimum wage, provident fund, insurance, old-age pensions, housing, health, education, and just about everything a citizen could expect from a responsible company. Similarly, companies like Premjee Foundation (Wipro) have chosen the backward region of North-east Karnataka to kick off the pilot phase of the Learning Guarantee Programme. The Foundation is working in partnership with the government of Karnataka and Andhra Pradesh.

Ambuja Foundation (Gujarat Ambuja Cement Ltd.) has initiated a project in the Sourastra region of Gujarat to help villagers in generating livelihood, natural resource management and community development. The Foundation has helped in the construction of water harvesting structures, dams, and other structures like culverts and percolation tanks.

CSR Activities of the TATA Group

Some of the prominent CSR activities of TATA Group are as follows:

1. Curative and preventive health services were rendered to 295,705 community members.
2. Scholarships for higher studies were awarded to 891 Students.

3. School infrastructure was developed for 100 schools.
4. Vocational training was imparted to 1048 youths.
5. Technical Training was provided to 1542 youths.
6. The green cover was increased by planting 290,850 trees.
7. Potable water solutions with support from the Sumant Moolgaonkar Development Foundation (SMDF) provided to 100 villages.
8. Donations (Including donations of vehicles) to help 52 NGO's for various social programs: 2,90,60,279

Apart from the above TATA group has also contributed immensely in the area of Women Empowerment and development of the rural area, for example: TATA steel has adopted the corporate citizenship Index, TATA business excellence Model and the TAT Index for sustainable development.TAT steel spends 5-7 per cent of its profits after tax on several CSR initiatives. Tata steel uses its skills and resources to give back to the community a fair share of the product of its efforts. Tata Steel is among the few Indian companies to be invited to join the UN-sponsored Global Compact Forum. Tata Steel's CSR initiatives are spread across areas such as environmental management, employee relations, economic development, civic amenities, and community services, population management, sports and adventure, health care, response to natural calamities, education, arts and culture, and social welfare. Over 500 self-help groups are currently operating under various poverty alleviation programs; out of which over 200 are engaged in activities of income generation through micro-enterprises. Women empowerment programs through self-help groups have been extended to 700 villages. For providing potable water to rural communities 2600 tube wells have been installed for the benefit of over 4 lakh people.

CSR activities of the ITC Limited

ITC is the only company in the world to be carbon positive, water positive and solid waste recycling positive. Environmental Initiatives of ITC Limited

- Carbon positive -seven years in a row
- Water positive- ten years in a row
- Solid waste recycling positive from last five years.

Social Initiatives of ITC Limited

- Generates livelihood for 5 million people
- ITC's e-Chaupal benefits over four million farmers.
- ITC's farm and forestry initiative have greened over 125000 hectares of barren land creating 56 million person-days of employment.
- ITC's watershed development program brings water to over 90000 hectares of land which are dry and water-stressed areas.
- Imparting education to farmers, women, children and other uneducated backward classes

Empowering the differently-abled

- ITC gives a fair chance to the differently-abled persons to earn a livelihood.
- ITC have employed over 100 differently abled persons to jobs like housekeeping, tele-working, bakeries and also as musicians.
- The company provides these people with special training and equipments to deal with their day to day work.
- ITC has been awarded 'NCPEDP shell Helen Keller award' to their hotels for their outstanding work.

INTEL, first and foremost, to expose that larger population to the use of the computer may be in the classroom, in the community, in higher, secondary and primary education. For this INTEL used a multi- pronged approach involving premier institutions, governments, universities; interacting at the policy.

Background and concept note: The ocean-based Blue Economy

The ocean-based Blue Economy (BE) is the next sunrise sector for development experts in India. With exactly 7517 kilometers long coastal line, India has a unique maritime position. The country has 12 major ports and 187 non-major ports, handling about 1400 million tons of cargo every year, as 95 per cent of India's trade by volume transits by sea. The coastal economy supports over 4 million fisher folk and coastal communities. BE contributes approx. 4% to the national GDP, which if studied in well organised manner can be enhanced to 12 to 15% of entire GDP.

India's blue economy comprises of the entire resources system in the ocean, economic infrastructure in marine, maritime and onshore coastal zones within country's legal jurisdiction.

Marine based economic development is also expected to reduce environmental risks and mitigate ecological challenges. As a result, efficient utilization of resources will enable us to achieve balanced socioeconomic development.

Given the pretext, India's vast marine interests occupies a crucial potential position in India's economic growth. The Government of India's vision of New India highlighted blue economy as one of the ten core dimensions of growth. According to the draft policy framework, India's approach to maximising the blue economy's socioeconomic potential includes a framework for: proper measurement of blue economy activities and their contribution to national income, ensuring the welfare, safety, and livelihood of fishermen in coastal areas, innovation to ensure zero waste, low carbon technologies, and securing balanced international engagement.

India has been showing interest in strengthening all the three pillars of the BE, namely, security, sustainability and economic prosperity.

Like the oceans, investment and growth in India's blue economy is limitless. With the right plan and proper initiatives by the government and private stakeholders, this conglomerate of sub-sectors has the potential to grow exponentially thereby giving an edge to India in trade, tourism, security and inclusive development.

Facts about the Blue Economy

- The worldwide ocean economy is valued at around US$1.5 trillion per year.
- Eighty per-cent of global trade by volume is carried by sea.
- 350 million jobs world-wide are linked to fisheries.
- By 2025 it is estimated that 34% of crude oil production will come from offshore fields.
- Aquaculture is the fastest growing food sector and provides about 50% of fish for human consumption.

India and the Blue Economy

There is much potential for India if it leverages on the blue economy. The Indian Ocean Region is abundant with resources, particularly in the sectors of fisheries, aquaculture, ocean energy, sea-bed mining and minerals, and provides tremendous economic opportunities to develop marine tourism and shipping activities.

Way Forward for Indian on Blue Economy

The Indian Ocean region needs a sustainable and inclusive framework for international partnerships. Countries in the region need to not only coordinate and manage the growing security challenges in the region but also realize the substantial economic potential the Indian Ocean area presents. India has significantly upped its development efforts in India's commitment to strengthen its cooperation with the regional partners and build a sustainable ocean economy aligns well with its domestic mega-modernisation projects that will enable the nation to harness the full potential of the Ocean based Blue Economy.

A related term of blue economy is ocean economy but despite the two being used interchangeably they are different from each other. Ocean economy focuses on use of ocean resources and is aimed at empowering the economic system of the ocean. While the blue economy goes beyond viewing the ocean economy solely as a mechanism of economic growth

The other term is green economy where the economy is aimed at reducing environmental risks, and that aims for sustainable development without degrading the environment. It is closely related with ecological economics.

Therefore, the blue economy is a part of the green economy. During the Rio+20 Summit in June 2012, Pacific small island developing states stated that, for them, "a green economy was in fact a blue economy".